PROTECTING YOURSELF
ONLINE

PROTECTING YOURSELF

ONLINE

The Definitive Resource on Safety, Freedom, and Privacy in Cyberspace

Robert B. Gelman with
Stanton McCandlish and
MEMBERS OF THE
Electronic Frontier Foundation

HarperEdge
An Imprint of HarperSanFrancisco

The following publishers have generously given permission to use extended quotations from copyrighted works. From *Everybody's Guide to the Internet,* by Adam Gaffin. Copyright © 1994–1998. Reprinted with permission by MIT Press, Cambridge, MA. From *Wired Magazine,* 2.03, "The Economy of Ideas," by John Perry Barlow. Copyright © 1994–1998. Reprinted with permission by Wired Magazine Group, Inc. All rights reserved. From "Civil Liberties in Cyberspace," by Mitch Kapor. Copyright © 1990–1998. Reprinted with permission by Scientific American, Inc. All rights reserved.

HarperCollins Web Site: *http://www.harpercollins.com/harperedge*

HarperCollins®, ♣®, and HarperSanFrancisco™, and HarperEdge™ are trademarks of HarperCollins Publishers Inc.

FIRST EDITION

Designed by Jessica Shatan

Library of Congress Cataloging-in-Publication Data

Gelman, Robert B.
    Protecting yourself online : the definitive resource on safety, freedom, and privacy in cyberspace / Robert B. Gelman with Stanton McCandlish and members of the Electronic Frontier Foundation. — 1st ed.
        p.   cm.
    Includes index
    ISBN: 0–06–251512–8
    1. Computer networks — Law and legislation — United States. 2. Privacy, Right of — United States. 3. Computer networks — Security measures — United States. I. McCandish, Stanton. II. Electronic Frontier Foundation. III. Title.
KF390. 5. C6 G45 1998
342.73'0858—dc21   97–032422

98 99 00 01 02 ❖/RRD (H) 10 9 8 7 6 5 4 3 2 1

This book is dedicated to the memory of my parents,
Sidney and Jeanne Gelman,
who were great teachers of the value of rights and responsibility,
and who taught in the most effective manner: by example.

Contents

Acknowledgments   ix

Foreword by Esther Dyson   xi

Introduction   xv

Chapter 1
Your Role on the Electronic Frontier:
Determining the Future of the Internet   1

Chapter 2
Free Expression and Censorship Online:
Reconciling Individual Liberties and Community Standards   19

Chapter 3
Privacy, Anonymity, and Secure Communications: Safeguarding
Sensitive Personal and Business Data in the Information Age   35

Chapter 4

Copyrights, Licenses, Trademarks, and Patents:
Protecting Intellectual Property Online   **85**

Chapter 5

The Code of Online Conduct? Learning Netiquette, Fighting Spam,
Recognizing Spoof Email, Dealing with Hackers and Crackers,
Treating Viruses, Spotting Scams, and Ensuring Equality   **115**

Chapter 6

Beyond the Frontier   **169**

Appendix   **175**

Contributors   **189**

Index   **191**

Acknowledgments

This book is a distillation of the ideas and words of many bright, dedicated individuals, a number of whom are affiliated with the Electronic Frontier Foundation (EFF). However, this work wouldn't have been possible were it not for the prior efforts of Stanton McCandlish, EFF's program director and the primary architect of the EFF Web site. His tireless efforts in creating this world-class library of information have not only made it easy for me to produce this book, but have also made EFF's site one of the four most linked-to sites on the World Wide Web.

I also want to thank Lori Fena of EFF and Michael Gosney of Verbum, Inc., for persevering in support of this project and the advancement of electronic communication.

Foreword

Welcome to *Protecting Yourself Online,* the first guide from the Electronic Frontier Foundation. We hope this book will be useful to you as you enter the empowering new world of online communication. There's a wealth of information in here—and much more "out there" in the Web sites we point to. After all, one benefit of the Net over a book is that it's infinitely expandable and constantly updated.

However, this book deals with some issues that will persist, even as the particulars of how we deal with them may change. Who is this "we"? It's all of us: the Electronic Frontier Foundation (EFF), governments, you, other people online, and purveyors of online services and content. Unfortunately, a lot of incomplete and even inaccurate information may have already reached you via the traditional media about the nature and extent of Internet problems such as fraud, virus propagation, and access of adult materials.

We seek to address those concerns in nonjudgmental ways, allowing you to evaluate how serious the threats they pose are to you, and offering you choices in methods for dealing with them. In fact, facilitating your "choice" is the underlying theme of the book, and of the work of EFF itself. We're here to provide solid, factual information to

individuals, businesses, and those involved in the regulation of the
new media about the realities involved therein.

The Electronic Frontier Foundation was founded in 1990 by
Mitch Kapor and John Perry Barlow, with involvement from John
Gilmore. John Barlow and John Gilmore are still active, though
Mitch is now "retired." The initial impetus in 1990 was to defend
Steve Jackson, owner of a computer game company who lost his business to overaggressive FBI agents when they suspected one of his
employees of "cracking"—breaking into other people's computers
over the Net. (He was eventually vindicated in court; see Chapter 5.)
Kapor, Barlow, and Gilmore got involved in his defense because they
believed that the legal authorities were overly aggressive—a result, in
part, of their fear of this new medium. The three launched the
Foundation as a defense fund and as a vehicle to educate the "authorities" about the Net. One of EFF's first activities was sponsorship of
the Computers, Freedom, and Privacy conference (now approaching
its eighth year), which gathered not just "our" side but an impressive
group of participants from the police, FBI, NSA, and the court system.

As time passed, we decided we needed to educate the people who
make the laws as well as those who *enforce* them. To do so more effectively, we moved to Washington, D.C., from our initial home in
Mitch Kapor's offices in Cambridge, Massachusetts. We had, almost
despite ourselves, became a full-fledged Beltway player, trying to
influence government legislation (though officially we were educating, not lobbying). But our hearts weren't in it. Mitch didn't like
Washington much and was withdrawing from the organization. Our
former executive director, Jerry Berman, left to start his own organization, the Center for Democracy and Technology, which now works
together with EFF in Washington on common issues such as privacy.
EFF itself picked up and moved to San Francisco. I became chairman
on the condition that we could find a good executive director to do
the real work. We found Lori Fena, a software entrepreneur who had

sold her company and was eager to apply her entrepreneurial talents to something socially beneficial. Whether it was two women running the place or the California influence, EFF fundamentally changed its focus from keeping the government out of the Net to figuring out how to build appropriate governance from within.

We do want rules; we just don't want rules imposed by centralized powers that tend to flout their own values, at times in secret. Instead of telling the government to keep out, we're fostering initiatives that will let individuals perform some of the tasks of Net governance—most notably, the TRUSTe initiative (see Appendix). With the help of such initiatives, people will be able to protect their own privacy while businesses foster commerce.

We're leading the fight for freedom of speech on the Net not just by arguing against censorship, but also by promoting the notion that people should be able to control the content they (and their children) receive. Overall, the EFF is a good model of the sort of organizations you'll find online. It's not a democracy, ruled by votes and opinion polls; it's a self-appointed voice in the discussion. We're more interested in gathering adherents by persuasion and illumination than in merely representing existing opinion.

The board of the Electronic Frontier Foundation follows our initial tradition. We're not a representative government; we're a group of people who have strong opinions—not always in consensus—about how the Net should develop. Whether you support us or criticize us, please know that we're trying to *persuade* you, not *rule* you. This book is intended to give you some of the tools and knowledge you'll need to think the tough questions through so that you can then act for yourself.

Welcome to the new frontier!

—ESTHER DYSON
Chairman, Electronic Frontier Foundation

Introduction

"Technology is neither good nor bad in its rough state. It's really how
we use it, as individuals, as corporations, and as government—how
we want to try to regulate it—that adds or reduces value."

LORI FENA, EFF EXECUTIVE DIRECTOR

Change happens. Ironically, it's one of the few constants in our lives. It's
surprising, then, how difficult it is for us to deal with all types of change.
We feel safe and comfortable with the status quo, yet we've been
seduced into a love affair with advancing technology. In the late twentieth century, that attraction has turned into a virtual addiction. Our
entertainment cravings lean toward high-definition virtual-reality TV.
Our need for convenience requires our automobiles to self-diagnose,
our microwave ovens to bake, rotate, and clean themselves. Our lust for
communication, perhaps the most extravagant of all, has brought us to
where it's possible to receive an email message from a handheld communicator, delivered via a Web page that arrives in our moving car by
cellular fax machine!

New technologies are reaching the market so fast that the progress has our heads spinning, and there's no sign of this tide ebbing. Indeed, the difference between evolution and revolution is little more than a matter of degree. While this may be evolution we're undergoing, it's so accelerated that its effect is more like revolution. What's unnerving is the fact that this revolution is proliferating for the most part unguided. Much of the development in computers and communications over the past two decades has surprised even the industry leaders who've benefited most from it.

Perhaps you're even a bit surprised to find yourself reading this book. If you feel as if most of the world's technological progress has been transpiring without you, or at least without your participation, you're not alone. Fueled by healthy technology markets, and humankind's thirst for the "new," the action seems to have started without the involvement of the majority of us.

Those employed by, or in the direct path of, emerging technologies have come to accept as normal the steep curve of learning and the adoption of new tools. Those of us not so directly influenced by the march of techno-progress may find ourselves on the sidelines, watching more or less helplessly as our culture dives headlong into who-knows-what. Some of these agents of change arrive surreptitiously, like Trojans in a wooden horse, in products and services we're already familiar with. Change is easier to accept and even welcome when it arrives in this manner. The first wireless phones to hit the consumer market, for example, were a welcome advance; it was easy to accept that the confining tether had been eliminated, never mind the fact that we'd begun to broadcast our conversations on open airwaves. The incremental advances over previous product versions smoothed the way for cellular phones in the car and other wireless devices.

The same process has been going on in numerous consumer-product categories—notably computers, the biggest tidal wave Western civilization has had to deal with since the harnessing of electricity. "Zap!"—we were caught unprepared for the changes to our lives that followed.

Computers have always been a communication tool—that is, communication between computer users. When we discovered that the interactive process could be enhanced if computers were directly connected to one another, that communication expanded. At first the link-up was accomplished with a "dumb" terminal and the all-powerful "mainframe"; then desktop computers (and their users) learned to share information; and finally, the Internet was born, a network of networks potentially linking every single desktop on the planet. To say that the Internet has "mushroomed" into our lives

> "Computers in the future may weigh no more than 1.5 tons."
> **POPULAR MECHANICS,**
> **1949**

would be a fine analogy. The growth happened right under the noses of those who were planning a somewhat different future, and it happened relatively overnight and without commercial cultivation (at least at first).

If this sounds more like a description of evolution than revolution to you, you're correct—so far. But the media flood tide of the late twentieth century has left us swimming in ever higher and faster waves of information. In his book *Data Smog,* David Shenk points out that "for nearly 100,000 years leading up to this century, information technology has been an unambiguous virtue as a means of sustaining and developing culture. . . . Because of information, we understand more about how to overcome the basic challenges of life. . . . Our citizens are freer, thanks to a wide dissemination of information that has empowered the individual. Dangerous superstitions and false notions have been washed away: Communicating quickly with people helps to overcome our fear of them and diminishes the likelihood of conflict." Shenk goes on to point out that as our media have evolved—through the drum, smoke signal, cave painting, horse, town crier, carrier pigeon, newspaper, photograph, telegraph, tele-phone, radio, and film—our capacity to process information has diminished in relation to the amount of information available.

Nonetheless, as more of society comes to depend on computers and electronic communication, you may feel the need to use these tools too. But just as the transition from agrarian to industrial society was not without its difficulties, the jump from industrial to informa-tion society has resulted in cultural shock waves now felt globally. We may discover the cures to serious threats from disease; we may put probes and soon humans on other planets; but we still don't deal well with change in our lives. The changes brought on by new communi-cations technology and the advent of digital media have presented us, as a society, with questions (as yet unanswered) as profound as any in our history, and have brought to the fore other questions that have gone unanswered throughout history—questions about identity, ve-racity, privacy, ownership, and the very nature of our changing civi-lization. Many of the institutions we've developed to serve us also find it difficult to meet some of the challenges of new technology, as the curve of progress sweeps upward on an ever-steeper path.

Our Newest Frontier

At first it was only the "nerds" and "geeks" of the digital revolution who stood on the frontier and then ventured into uncharted terri-tory. Much like the pioneers who left the safety of their homes and spread west through North America in the eighteenth and nineteenth centuries, these early explorers on the "electronic frontier" assumed the responsibility for charting this territory, then building the infra-structure for the civilization to follow. Instead of horses, hammers, shovels, and firearms, they packed software and modems. Who knows? Perhaps your grandchildren and their descendants will be reading about Tim Berners-Lee, Mark Andreesen, Bill Gates, and Al Gore in the very books that cover Columbus, Sir Francis Drake, and Abraham Lincoln!

You probably don't see yourself as one of these pioneers; indeed, you may not even recognize their names. You may be part of the second generation, coming to settle the electronic frontier now that it no longer requires technical credentials. Maybe you resisted getting a computer, had no interest in going online, finally succumbing only because you felt you *had* to. If so, you're among the settlers who will comprise the second wave, bringing culture and the values of civilization to the new territory. Or perhaps you're simply curious, or looking for a new business opportunity. Certainly the electronic frontier is poised for a gold rush of its own.

This new frontier is not without its outlaws and ambushes, to say nothing of lynch mobs and highwaymen. If you believe the reports in the papers and on television, you're well justified in being reluctant to venture here. Will porn-peddlers jump out and accost you? Will hackers steal your bank account? Is it really worth all the cost and hassle to get your family online? The answers to these questions (and a lot more) await you in the pages that follow.

The truth about how the Net will unfold probably lies somewhere between the hyperbolic sound bites warning of a pornography-saturated medium and the libertarian cries for a totally free-form global network. This new place, sometimes referred to as "cyberspace," is where information of every kind imaginable exists, continually changing, expanding, "morphing." It's a place where learning, connection with others, and entertainment happen. It's a place where commerce is facilitated at a fraction of the cost of more traditional means. Most amazingly, it's a place of a sort that's never before existed: one where the ideas and concerns of any individual can be accessed by nearly anyone else, without the mediation of a publisher or producer.

It may still sound like science-fiction fodder to some, but once you've experienced the ease and immediacy of email, the interactivity of the World Wide Web, or the depth and breadth of the numerous online services, you'll understand what all the excitement's about. The coincidental emergence of several technologies has opened a threshold for us to step through, a portal into the next phase of our civilization. But while those technologies have opened a portal, they haven't left us a roadmap. They haven't posted directional signs or rules of the road. They've simply left us at the edge of this new frontier, with all its mystery, danger, and promise.

Armed with solid information on the potential dangers in being online today—*and* how to deal with them—you'll soon be discovering new worlds of personal interest and business potential and communities of affinity in the online realm that will make it well worth the risk of pioneering. We hope you'll find this book to be a useful guide in doing so, whether you're a businessperson, an educator, a legislator, or a concerned parent.

Using This Book

The central difference between the passive electronic media of the mid–twentieth century and the new media is *interactivity.* That's what enables genuine two-way communication. And that's where those who are comfortable with the old way of things start to get *un*comfortable—sometimes even fearful. As you'd expect, the best decisions are generally made not in an atmosphere of fear but rather in an environment of enlightenment and understanding. It's fear based on ignorance, we believe, that's been the basis for the many repressive and regressive laws that have been handed down in the past few years. Therefore, one of our primary goals at the Electronic Frontier Foundation (EFF) is to bring all relevant aspects of these technological issues to light, to give legislators a clear understanding of that which they're being asked to regulate (indeed, we do support legal participation, as long as it's characterized by clarity and consistency). We also hope to bring to light the practical limits of legal remedies in a realm where geographical jurisdictions simply don't exist.

Those of you ready to step across the threshold are facing an exciting and potentially satisfying experience, but not one that much resembles television or radio. It seeks your involvement, your questions, your ideas, your opinions, your activism. It offers you the opportunity to learn from the largest library of knowledge humanity has ever assembled. It allows you to add to that library with your own knowledge and opinions. It also harbors misinformation, and mischievous and criminal activity to be avoided. Danger on the new frontier? Yes. Worth the risk to go there? We certainly think so. Armed with the knowledge in this book, you'll be prepared to deal with the challenges. For as surely as computers aren't television, this isn't just another book about the Internet.

One thing that traditional news media are very good at is creating alarm. In fact, they've made fear one of their primary tools for maintaining audience interest and attention. That said, you've probably heard about things like computer viruses, scam artists, pornographers, thieves, and other predators—a host of bad guys just waiting to get you online. Such stories command good ratings points for the broadcast media and sell copies of (and advertising in) publications. How much truth is in them? That depends on the medium and the particular story you're referring to, of course, but in general they're blown out of proportion.

If we were to make a general statement that put the prevalence of these "evils" into a more realistic perspective, we'd have to say that they exist online in proportions approximating those of the physical world. The online world represents a microcosm of the world around us, with its knowledge, its wonder, and its darker side. You wouldn't let the existence of so-called adult bookstores keep you or your family from walking down the street, nor should you let the existence of adult Web sites keep you or your family from using the World Wide Web. The fact that someone might make an unwanted call to your home doesn't stop you from answering the phone, nor should the possibility that someone may send you junk email keep you from having an email account.

In every case, these problems represent questions of social importance to the online community and to the rest of the world. There are choices available to (most of) us as to how we'll overcome these problems when we face them. The basic knowledge offered in these pages will equip you to avoid many of the potential problems and, for those that can't be avoided, inform you as to possible solutions and help you see what course of action makes sense for you.

The book is divided into six chapters. As you proceed through them, you'll get a sense of how we got where we are today with the new media, discover why the issues we're grappling with have greater importance than their face value suggests, and learn about your role in helping to decide what the future will look like. You'll also look in some depth at the controversial (and the mundane) issues that are of concern to people online, whether they be businesspeople, educators, or families. These include how to protect yourself and your family from unwanted communication, how private your email really is, what information is gathered about you by Web sites, and much more. You'll find many comparisons to controversies in the traditional media, and quotes from numerous contributors to the EFF online archives. Chapter 6 is an "editorial" of sorts: it offers a point of view on how the Net and other new media can reach their potential, and points out where there's a genuine need for government involvement in solutions. At the end of each chapter (and in the Appendix), you'll find Internet links for locating more information online about most of the subjects discussed here.

And finally, we've developed a Web site specifically for you, the reader of this book: *http://www.eff.org/guide.* This digest site will help you to identify important resources within and outside of the EFF on issues of concern to you, your family, or your organization.

This book is just one of many resources available to help you as you venture into the new media. It's our hope that with the information you find here, you'll develop your own viewpoint on how to best protect yourself online. Use the tools well, and you'll be prepared for the adventure that awaits you on the electronic frontier.

ONE | YOUR ROLE ON THE
ELECTRONIC
FRONTIER

Determining the
Future of the Internet

The Internet, though the main focus of this book, is not the limit of its scope. Cellular phones, pagers, and handheld communications devices are all part of the topography of the electronic frontier. Each has its own unique properties and carries its own set of challenges for us as users, developers, or regulators.

To understand our respective roles in the realm of cyberspace, it helps to know a little about what the terrain is like here—what makes up the infrastructure, the regulatory environment, the user-base. As we survey that terrain, a little history is helpful.

How the Internet Came to Be

In the 1960s, researchers began experimenting with linking computers to each other and to people through telephone hookups, using funds from the U.S. Defense Department's Advanced Research Projects Agency (ARPA). ARPA wanted to see if computers in different locations could be linked using a new technology known as "packet switching." This technology, in which data meant for another location is broken up into little pieces, each with its own "forwarding address," had the promise of letting several users share just one communications line. Just as important, from ARPA's viewpoint, was that this allowed for creation of networks that could automatically route data around downed circuits or computers. ARPA's goal was not the creation of today's international computer-using community, but development of a data network that could survive a nuclear attack.

Previous computer-networking efforts had required a line between each computer on the network, sort of like a one-track train route. The packet system allowed for creation of a data highway in which large numbers of vehicles could essentially share the same lane. Each packet was given the computer equivalent of a map and a time stamp so that it could be sent to the right destination, where it would then be reassembled into a message the computer or a human could use.

This system allowed computers to share data and the researchers to exchange electronic mail (or *email*). In itself, email was something of a revolution, offering the ability to send detailed letters at the speed of a phone call.

As this system, known as ARPANet, grew, some enterprising college students (and one high-schooler) developed a way to use it to conduct online conferences. These started as science-oriented discussions, but they soon branched out into virtually every other field as people recognized the power of being able to "talk" to hundreds, or even thousands, of people around the country.

In the 1970s, ARPA helped support the development of rules, or "protocols," for transferring data between different types of computer networks. These "internet" (from "internetworking") protocols made it possible to develop the worldwide Net we have today, which links all sorts of computers across national boundaries. By the close of the 1970s, links had been developed between ARPANet and counterparts in other countries. The world was now tied together in a computer web.

In the 1980s, this network of networks, which became known collectively as the Internet, expanded at a phenomenal rate. Hundreds, then thousands, of colleges, research companies, and government agencies began to connect their computers to this worldwide Net. Some enterprising hobbyists and companies unwilling to pay the high costs of Internet access (or unable to meet stringent government regulations for access) learned how to link their own systems to the Internet, even if "only" for email and conferences. Some of these systems began offering access to the public. Now anybody with a computer and modem, persistence, and a small amount of money could tap into the world.

In the 1990s, the Net continues to grow at exponential rates. Some trend-watchers estimate that the volume of messages transferred through the Net grows 20 percent a month. In response, government and other users have tried in recent years to expand the Net itself. Once, the main Net "backbone" in the United States moved data at 56,000 bits per second. That proved too slow for the ever-increasing amounts of data being sent over it, and in recent years the maximum speed was increased to 1.5 million and then to 45 million bits per second. Even before the Net was able to reach that latter speed, however, Net experts were already figuring out ways to pump data at speeds of up to 2 billion bits per second—fast enough to send the entire *Encyclopedia Britannica* across the country in just one or two seconds. Another major change has been the development of commercial services that provide internetworking services at speeds comparable to those of the government system. In fact, what started as a government experiment is now largely a private enterprise.

How the Internet Works

The worldwide Net is actually a complex web of smaller regional networks. To understand the system, picture a modern network of transcontinental superhighways connecting large cities. From these large cities come smaller freeways and parkways that link small towns, whose residents travel on narrow residential roads.

The Net superhighway is the high-speed Internet. Connected to this are computers that use a particular system of transferring data at high speeds. In the United States, the major Internet computers theoretically can move data at rates of 45 million bits per second (compare this to the average home modem, which has a top speed of roughly 28,800 bits per second). Connected to the backbone computers are smaller networks serving particular geographical regions; these networks generally move data at speeds around 1.5 million bits per second. Feeding off these are even smaller networks or individual computers.

Unlike commercial networks (such as CompuServe or Prodigy), the Internet isn't run by a central computer or computers; its resources are to be found among thousands of individual computers. This is both its greatest strength and its greatest weakness. Because of this broad base, it's virtually impossible for the entire Net to crash at once; even if one computer shuts down, the rest of the network stays up. The design also reduces the cost for an individual or organization to get onto the network. However, thousands of connected computers can also make it difficult to navigate the Net and find what you want—especially since different computers may have different commands for plumbing their resources. It's only recently that Net users have begun to develop the sorts of navigational tools and "maps" that let neophytes get around without getting lost.

Nobody really knows how many computers and networks actually make up this Net. Some estimates say there are now as many as thirty thousand networks connecting nearly ten million computers and more than sixty million people around the world. Whatever the actual numbers, however, it's clear they're increasing.

The Net is more than just a technological marvel. It's human communication at its most fundamental level. The pace may be a little quicker when the messages race around the world in a few seconds, but surfing the Net isn't much different from attending a large and interesting party. You'll see things in cyberspace that will make you laugh; you'll see things that will anger you. You'll read silly little snippets and new ideas that make you think. You'll make new friends and meet people you wish would just go away. And you'll do it all in a community that transcends state lines and national borders.

Major network providers continue to work on ways to make it easier for users of one network to communicate with those of another. For example, work is under way on a system for providing a universal user directory—a "white pages" in which you could look up somebody's email address. This connectivity trend will likely speed up in coming years as users begin to demand seamless network access, much as telephone users now can dial almost anywhere in the world without worrying about how many phone companies have to connect their calls.

The Internet today is indeed far more than it was just a couple of years ago. In its infancy, everything users accomplished on the Net was text-based. Applications such as Gopher and Telnet enabled people to log on to a remote host computer via the Net and then execute commands and view and download files residing there. WAIS (Wide Area Information Search) enabled users to do some searching for topics that were of interest to them, although the indexing was comparatively superficial. And of course email was among the first (and is still the most popular) of Internet applications.

All of these programs are still used in some areas today, although they've been largely supplanted by newer multimedia technologies such as the World Wide Web, which brings a graphic interface and other media to your desktop. In 1989, Tim Berners-Lee, while working at the European Particle Physics Laboratory (CERN), invented the World Wide Web. This initiative for the first time enabled direct hyperlinking from one source of information to another, regardless of what computer that information resided on and where in the world it was located.

Soon thereafter, an application known as Mosaic was developed by Mark Andreesen and his associates at the National Center for Supercomputing Applications at the University of Illinois in Urbana-Champaign. Mosaic was the first "browser," or graphic interface for viewing the World Wide Web. Since that time, literally dozens of other browsers have come along, each with its own particular style of transforming the digital information on Web servers into multimedia for your desktop computer. More important, the underlying technologies, such as HTML (Hypertext Markup Language) and Java (a cross-platform programming language), have enabled these browsers to do much more than simply present text and graphics. Today's browsers can present audio, video, animation, video-conferencing, and more, depending on the speed of your connection and your computer's processor. Web servers can customize pages in real time, and groupware applications now allow document-sharing, multipoint conferencing, and more. Just around the corner, new technologies that allow "pushing" will enable you to receive "channels" of selectable information that will arrive at your computer automatically as updates happen. "Bots" (short for "knowbots," which comes from "robots") or other autonomous artificially intelligent agents will scour the Net for information on your behalf. And who knows the possibilities for the long term?

What the Internet Means for the Future

A new world is arising in the vast web of digital electronic media that connects us. Computer-based communications media are becoming the basis of new communities of a different sort. These communities, lacking a single, fixed geographical location, make up the first settlements on the electronic frontier. Digital networks offer a tremendous potential to empower individuals in an ever-overpowering world. However, these communications networks are also the subject of significant debate concerning governance and freedom.

While well-established legal principles and the standards of physical communities give structure and coherence to uses of conventional media such as newspapers, books, and telephones, the new digital media don't so easily fit into existing frameworks. What jurisdiction's laws can hope to apply justly to a medium that's both nowhere and everywhere at the same time? Serious conflicts come about as the law struggles to define its application in a context where fundamental notions of speech, property, and place take profoundly new forms. People sense both the promises and the threats inherent in the use of new computer and communications technologies, even as they struggle to master or simply cope with them in the workplace and the home. Some of those promises and threats are encapsulated in the following questions:

- How do we balance intellectual property rights with the free flow of information?

- How do we simultaneously provide for free expression and allow individuals to shield themselves or their children from material they find offensive?

- How do we determine which country's laws, if any, sensibly have jurisdiction over media that involve global communications?

- How do we protect privacy and security while fostering accountability and responsibility?

- How do we ensure that legislators, access providers, and network users don't stifle speech they disagree with?

What's at Stake for Individuals

Since the beginning of history, humankind has faced questions related to the trade-offs between the liberty of individuals and the needs of society. The advent of digital technology has brought these trade-offs into a conflict more intense than ever, because now anyone with online access has the power to communicate quickly and inexpensively with great numbers of people all over the world—and to infringe the rights of others, to invade privacy, to misinform, and to collect personal information and redistribute it worldwide!

In traditional personal media, such as the postal services, there's a natural barrier—one constructed of service fees and the cost in time and materials involved in broadly distributing your message—that serves to protect privacy and to limit the ease with which you express yourself. In electronic communication, that barrier is displaced, and the ease of automatically reaching large numbers of people with your message is consequently multiplied.

In recent times, we've seen the Internet give voice to dissidents in repressive countries, bringing human rights abuses to the attention of the world. We've seen artists who haven't met the criteria for commercial acceptance (specifically, the criterion of mass appeal) find an audience for their writing, imagery, or music. And we've seen entrepreneurs with great ideas, but little in the way of investment capital, discover practical, low-cost ways of bringing their products or services to market. And this barely scratches the surface.

Given the frequency with which new products are arriving online, it's not hard to envision networking interfaces (those means by which we interact with the computer) that will allow us to remotely control our home appliances (starting up the oven at home before we leave the office, for example), enable us to meet in virtual worlds, or give us access to all our personal financial information and allow us to conduct transactions from anyplace on the planet—*even when we're not at a computer!*

These innovations are just over the horizon, but if they're to become practical and acceptable to us as consumers, we'll want to be sure that the "keys" that give access to sensitive personal data belong to us alone and are in our control. And we'll want to be confident that the transmission of private information can't be intercepted en route in a way that allows for abuse. We'll also want to know who's gathering data about our online visits and preferences, and what they'll be doing with that data. And we'll want to know all these things in advance so that we can choose whether or not we wish to give information or have a profile created about us. Until key questions such as these are answered satisfactorily on a global basis, great advances will be delayed for months or years, some perhaps never reaching the consumer market.

What's at Stake for Businesses

Much business is conducted directly over the public networks today. Software is distributed, news is delivered, banking is transacted, book and music sales are finalized. In some communities you can even place pizza-delivery and taxicab orders over the Net. These and other activities are rapidly building cyberspace into a significant marketplace. But the growth of this powerful medium on behalf of business in general has been severely limited, in large part because of the lack of standards for transactions and data security. Several agencies and standards groups, along with governments worldwide, are wrestling with these issues today, in an effort to open up the possibilities for safe world commerce over the Net.

Some of the same concerns that affect individuals are the keys to making Internet commerce more viable. As a business operator, you want to be safe from fraud, and you want assurance that neither your competitors nor someone out to get you can access your sensitive information, that your very operation is safe from intrusion via the Net. And what about your customers? If you invest in serving them via the electronic media, will they take advantage of the service, or will they keep to the old ways of doing business out of fear of being ripped off or of having their account abused somehow?

Standards need to be developed for ethical online business practices that maximize the potential of the medium while protecting personal and organizational civil rights. While these issues aren't necessarily at odds, there are trade-offs for any set of practices that might be agreed upon. But those trade-offs are a thing of the future: we haven't even been able to figure out who (or what body) should make these determinations. That's where you, the private citizen or business operator, come in. You have the opportunity to determine your own fate on the electronic frontier if you envision the possibilities, learn how to make your voice heard, and support the establishment of sensible standards of conduct online.

The same goes for educators, some of whom were among the earliest settlers in cyberspace. The Net is still a tool through which the academic community conducts distance learning and shares resources and knowledge, but no longer is that tool limited to the halls of higher education. Telecollaboration now allows top-level information to reach communities that were too remote for such things just a year or two ago. Specialized medical expertise can be transmitted from an Ivy League research and teaching facility to a small hospital on a Native American reservation without much difficulty. Advanced farming techniques can be taught to eager students in Third World

countries. And adults in remote locations can gain a better understanding of different cultures, even as their children meet in online
worlds. This is the second phase of the Net's potential for education—and here too we've just scratched the surface.

What's at Stake for Legislators

With the technology and content of the electronic media changing
drastically every few months, legislators—along with Internet users
everywhere—are facing challenges unlike any they've had to address
before. For example, their constituents may be clamoring for protection from "spam" (unsolicited promotional email) or expressing out-
rage that their kids can access material they don't approve of. What
should their role be? How can they possibly keep up? The world is
being changed in such a fundamental and far-reaching manner by
the spread of the Net that it's not a question of *whether* legislators will
need to learn about it . . . only *when*. Regardless of the con-
stituency—be it local or national, democractic or monarchical—all
legislators will eventually face decisions that impact what happens
online. It's therefore essential that they have a basic understanding of
how these media work, how they've developed, and what they're
capable of. In addition, legislators need to understand the technological, legal, and personal issues that have been (and continue to be) of
concern to the community on and off the Net, as well as how current
solutions are being implemented.

Here is a nongeographical community that interacts with all geographical jurisdictions yet has its own standards of behavior, many
of which may be foreign to legislators, and may even seem to challenge their authority. That sort of challenge from an unknown
adversary could provoke fear in anyone, but legislators are in a position of too much responsibility to let fear be their guide. Basing
their decisions on an understanding of this new world, they must

exercise great courage in the pursuit of just answers to cyberspace conflicts.

Laws and case precedents that are being set today are extremely critical: they will either foster the potential of the wondrous new media and enhance our precious civil liberties, or they will limit those liberties and discourage the development of the most important tool in decades. That's an awesome responsibility! Unfortunately, there are too few tools available to give legislators a clear picture of the long-term implications of their decisions in this arena.

While this book doesn't pretend to go into these issues in the detail legislators will surely need, it offers an excellent introduction and serves as a guidepost to additional resources. Some of the key legal cases are analyzed or referenced in these pages, and a balanced array of sources of in-depth information are listed. There are tools here that the legislators among our readership can use to better serve constituents on many levels. For example, imagine being able to poll your constituents on an urgent issue, take the pulse of your district on a variety of topics prior to a campaign, or lobby your colleagues on actions of concern to you. All these things can be done now. Someday elections themselves may take place online. Indeed, the Net may be the greatest tool for democracy we've ever seen—*if* it reaches its potential. For that to happen, all legislators need to become involved now.

Guarding Frontier Outposts

Although the Electronic Frontier Foundation is proudly a civil liberties organization, it doesn't support an online realm without laws and enforcement procedures. On the contrary, for the public networks to become a civilized place for us in the future, we must follow in the footsteps of our ancestors, determining (as wisely as we're able) where to draw the line between acceptable and unacceptable behaviors. We must set out legal punishments that are reasonable and proportional to the infractions, and support fair and equitable enforcement of those laws. Where possible, we must deter criminal or antisocial behaviors with technological and social deterrents. And we must always attempt to protect precious rights by encouraging individual responsibility.

In July of 1990, Mitch Kapor (ex-CEO of Lotus) and John Perry Barlow (lyricist and cyber-activist) co-founded the Electronic Frontier Foundation with the publication of the following manifesto:

Across the Electronic Frontier
by Mitchell Kapor and John Perry Barlow

Over the last fifty years, the people of the developed world have begun to cross into a landscape unlike any which humanity has experienced before. It is a region without physical shape or form. It exists, like a standing wave, in the vast web of our electronic communications systems. It consists of electron states, micro-waves, magnetic fields, light pulses and thought itself.

It is familiar to most people as the "place" in which a long-distance telephone conversation takes place. But it is also the repository for all digital or electronically transferred information, and, as such, it is the venue for most of what is now commerce, industry, and broad-scale human interaction. William Gibson called this Platonic realm "Cyberspace," a name which has some currency among its present inhabitants.

Whatever it is eventually called, it is the homeland of the Information Age, the place where the future is destined to dwell.

In its present condition, Cyberspace is a frontier region, popu-lated by the few hardy technologists who can tolerate the austerity of its savage computer interfaces, incompatible communications protocols, proprietary barricades, cultural and legal ambiguities, and general lack of useful maps or metaphors.

Certainly, the old concepts of property, expression, identity, movement, and context, based as they are on physical manifestation, do not apply succinctly in a world where there can be none.

Sovereignty over this new world is also not well defined. Large institutions already lay claim to large fiefdoms, but most of the actual natives are solitary and independent, sometimes to the point of sociopathy. It is, therefore, a perfect breeding ground for both outlaws and vigilantes. Most of society has chosen to ignore the existence of this arising domain. Every day millions of people use ATMs and credit cards, place telephone calls, make travel reservations, and access information of limitless variety . . . all without any perception of the digital machinations behind these transactions.

Our financial, legal, and even physical lives are increasingly dependent on realities of which we have only dimmest awareness. We have entrusted the basic functions of modern existence to institutions we cannot name, using tools we've never heard of and could not operate if we had.

As communications and data technology continues to change and develop at a pace many times that of society, the inevitable conflicts have begun to occur on the border between Cyberspace and the physical world.

These are taking a wide variety of forms, including (but hardly limited to) the following:

I. Legal and Constitutional Questions

What is free speech and what is merely data? What is a free press without paper and ink? What is a "place" in a world without tangible dimensions? How does one protect property which has no physical form and can be infinitely and easily reproduced? Can the history of one's personal business affairs properly belong to someone else? Can anyone morally claim to own knowledge itself?

These are just a few of the questions for which neither law nor custom can provide concrete answers. In their absence, law enforcement agencies like the Secret Service and FBI, acting at the disposal of large information corporations, are seeking to create legal precedents which would radically limit Constitutional application to digital media.

The excesses of Operation Sun Devil[1] are only the beginning of what threatens to become a long, difficult, and philosophically obscure struggle between institutional control and individual liberty.

II. Future Shock

Information workers, forced to keep pace with rapidly changing technology, are stuck on "the learning curve of Sisyphus." Increasingly, they find their hard-acquired skills to be obsolete even before they've been fully mastered. To a lesser extent, the same applies to ordinary citizens who correctly feel a lack of control over their own lives and identities.

One result of this is a neo-Luddite resentment of digital technology from which little good can come. Another is a decrease in worker productivity ironically coupled to tools designed to enhance it. Finally, there is a spreading sense of alienation, dislocation, and helplessness in the general presence of which no society can expect to remain healthy.

III. The "Knows" and the "Know-Nots"

Modern economies are increasingly divided between those who are comfortable and proficient with digital technology and those who neither understand nor trust it. In essence, this development disenfranchises the latter group, denying them any possibility of citizenship in Cyberspace and, thus, participation in the future.

Furthermore, as policymakers and elected officials remain relatively ignorant of computers and their uses, they unknowingly abdicate most of their authority to corporate technocrats whose jobs do not include general social responsibility. Elected government is thus replaced by institutions with little real interest beyond their own quarterly profits.

> "We're not left-wing or right-wing, we're up-wing."
>
> **JOHN GILMORE,**
> EFF co-founder

We are founding the Electronic Frontier Foundation to deal with these and related challenges. While our agenda is ambitious to the point of audacity, we don't see much that these issues are being given the broad social attention they deserve. We were forced to ask, "If not us, then who?"

In fact, our original objectives were more modest. When we first heard about Operation Sun Devil and other official adventures into the digital realm, we thought that remedy could be derived by simply unleashing a few highly competent Constitutional lawyers upon the government. In essence, we were prepared to fight a few civil libertarian brush fires and go on about our private work.

However, examination of the issues surrounding these government actions revealed that we were dealing with the symptoms of a much larger malady, the collision between Society and Cyberspace.

We have concluded that a cure can lie only in bringing civilization to Cyberspace. Unless a successful effort is made to render that harsh and mysterious terrain suitable for ordinary inhabitants, friction between the two worlds will worsen. Constitutional protections, indeed the perceived legitimacy of representative government itself, might gradually disappear.

We could not allow this to happen unchallenged, and so arises

the Electronic Frontier Foundation. In addition to our legal inter-
ventions on behalf of those whose rights are threatened, we will:

• Engage in and support efforts to educate both the general
  public and policymakers about the opportunities and challenges posed by developments in computing and telecommunications.

• Encourage communication between the developers of technology, government, corporate officials, and the general
  public in which we might define the appropriate metaphors
  and legal concepts for life in Cyberspace.

• And, finally, foster the development of new tools which
  will endow non-technical users with full and easy access to
  computer-based telecommunications.

One of us, Mitch Kapor, had already been a vocal advocate of
more accessible software design and had given considerable
thought to some of the challenges we now intend to meet.

The other, John Perry Barlow, is a relative newcomer to the
world of computing (though not to the world of politics) and is
therefore well equipped to act as an emissary between the magi-
cians of technology and the wary populace who must incorporate
this magic into their daily lives.

While we expect the Electronic Frontier Foundation to be a
creation of some longevity, we hope to avoid the sclerosis which
organizations usually develop in their efforts to exist over time.
For this reason we will endeavor to remain light and flexible,
marshalling intellectual and financial resources to meet specific
purposes rather than finding purposes to match our resources.
As is appropriate, we will communicate between ourselves and
with our constituents largely over the electronic Net, trusting self-

distribution and self-organization to a much greater extent than
would be possible for a more traditional organization.

We readily admit that we have our work cut out for us.
However, we are greatly encouraged by the overwhelming and
positive response which we have received so far. We hope the
Electronic Frontier Foundation can function as a focal point for
the many people of goodwill who wish to settle in a future as
abundant and free as the present.

Much has transpired since 1990. The Net has grown exponentially
in number of users, amount of information available, and the ways in
which that information is accessible. The rate at which these developments are happening has found many of us unprepared to deal with
the Net's changing conventions and applications. Reports in the press
about the presence of fraud, pornography, and other crimes have led
many to wonder whether the Net is worth the hassle and the potential danger lurking there. The answer to that is something you'll have
to determine for yourself. When you understand the true nature of
the controversies, and the solutions and protections available, we
think the answer will clearly be, "Yes, very much worth it."

To help you make that determination, we offer, in the next chapter, a critical look at the key issues involved in being online.

NOTE

1. On November 6, 1992, a group of people affiliated with the computer magazine
2600 were confronted by private security personnel, local police officers, and several
unidentified individuals. The group members were ordered to identify themselves and to
submit to searches of their personal property. Their names were recorded by the security
personnel and some of their property was confiscated. However, no charges were ever
brought against any of the individuals at the meeting.

The Secret Service didn't formally acknowledge its role in the November incident.
However, a security official and the Arlington County Police have said that Secret Service
agents were present and directed the activities of the private security personnel.

TWO | FREE EXPRESSION AND CENSORSHIP ONLINE

Reconciling Individual Liberties and Community Standards

"We believe in free speech at the source—and in the empowerment of any audience for that speech to control what they see."

ESTHER DYSON, EFF CHAIRMAN

The framers of the U.S. Constitution must have thought very highly of the value of free speech, protecting it in the first article of the Bill of Rights. ("Congress shall make no law . . . abridging the freedom of speech, or of the press.") They recognized that freedom of individual expression and a free press are the underpinnings of true democracy—a form of government that until then had been only an ideal.

The ability to communicate without fear of recrimination is something taken for granted by many of us in the United States these days, though less so elsewhere in the world. For many, the Internet is the first and only medium in which they've been able to experience such freedom, along with the power of mass communication. Its "newness" brings both exhilaration and trepidation. Yet the Net, cellular phones, and personal digital assistants are likely only the first of a wave of new media technologies that will change the way we communicate, learn, and interact in the near future.

Redefining "*Mass* Communication"

It wasn't long ago (1993) that the coming of the "info superhighway" was heralded with hype and promotion in a whole host of publications and on the cover of *TIME* magazine. We were led to expect hundreds of new channels of information and told that every library, school, hospital, and home would soon be connected to the Internet. And for the first time, seers predicted, we would all be potential publishers.

Just a few years later (with a lot more than a few hundred channels available to us), the Internet is viewed in many areas as a threat . . . because everyone *is* a publisher! Because an amazing amount of information—and, to a lesser degree, disinformation—*is* available instantly to every library, school, hospital, and home worldwide. What's delivered may not be well written; it may offend; it may contain radical personal opinions that are neither "nice" nor politically palatable. That's a frightening prospect to many. Unfortunately, people's fears have played out in the traditional media and in regulating bodies in ways that could impact long-standing individual rights in very damaging ways.

Although free speech issues have been at the center of political debate frequently since the Bill of Rights was written, we have to view them in a new light when considering the new electronic media.

Many of our earlier technological developments—the telephone, for example, which certainly wasn't considered by the authors of the Bill of Rights—furthered communication on a relatively small scale. Although telephone technology was revolutionary when it was introduced, and threatening to some users, phone conversations were likened by legislators to *private* speech and protected accordingly. And private speech it is: as a one-to-one medium, the telephone allows intimate two-way conversation. It certainly isn't well suited to reaching a mass audience. (If you've tried conference calls, you know what we mean.)

While the First Amendment addressed mass communication, the form of one-to-many communication that was on the minds of the Constitution's developers was the newspaper, which—like its descendants, film and broadcasting—projects from a central source to a wide audience. These traditional media have great power in the numbers they reach, yet they lack the intimacy and interactivity of the telephone and the Net. Even given the options for feedback—"op-ed" pages, letters to the editor, brief on-air editorial rebuttals—viewers and opponents never get close to "equal time."

The Net has radically changed mass communication practically overnight. The first many-to-many medium, it combines broadcasting and print media's power to reach large audiences with the telephone's intimacy and multidirectional flow. It's both powerful and personal.

It's also cheap in comparison with other forms of mass communication. If you want to start a newspaper, you've got to have many millions of dollars behind you. Even then, your chances of being successful are slim. Yet today, if you can get on the Net—and most people can—you can reach larger audiences than even the largest paper-and-ink newspapers.

This represents a radical shift in power. For the first time, average individuals can experience true freedom of the press. Any person or organization can reach a massive audience, without an editor to alter the message or make it "acceptable." This shift in power has sparked the fear of change that's so central to human nature (and, it follows, to corporate and institutional nature as well).

The Consequences of Widespread Freedom of the Press

> "The Internet interprets censorship as damage, and routes around it."[1]
>
> **JOHN GILMORE,**
> EFF co-founder

What we find available on the Internet mirrors what we find in the physical world, in some digital form. In both locations, we find wondrous libraries of science, culture, and humanity, as well as aspects of our society's darker side. It's true that people who want to publish or read "pornography" or "dangerous information" (such as bomb-making instructions) can do so on the Internet. However, these controversial modes of expression are also readily found in community libraries and bookstores across the country. They're protected under the First Amendment when they sit on a bookshelf, but they cause an uproar when discovered on the Net.

The uproar probably stems from the fear that such material will stream into one's home via the Net in the way television and radio programs do. If that were the case, there might be more cause for concern; we might want to restrict it, keep it from the eyes of our children, or limit its flow. But the truth is you have to go looking for this kind of content, and in many cases, you must prove your age or identity to access it, just as you would in an adult bookstore.

But the uproar sparked by controversial information on the Internet continues, underscored by the difficulty for the electorate, legislatures, and courts to set out guidelines by which existing laws can be better applied to the new media. Some of the legal and societal implications of free and widespread dissemination of information on the Internet are brought out in the following comments:

"Community Standards" and the Virtual Community
by Mike Godwin, EFF Counsel

In a landmark case, Robert and Carleen Thomas operated an adult-oriented BBS [an electronic "bulletin-board system" where users can post and download information] called Amateur Action BBS, in California. The operator of a BBS typically dedicates a computer and one or more phone lines at his home or business for the use of an online community. Each user calls up the BBS (using a modem, as if accessing the Internet) and leaves public messages that can be read by all other users, and/or private mail to be read by a particular user. A BBS, while generally a forum for those of similar interests, can also be a place to trade in computer files, programs, or images, including sexually explicit ones.

In the Thomas case, a Tennessee postal inspector, working with an assistant U.S. attorney in Memphis, became a member of the Thomas's BBS (at the regular fee of ninety-nine dollars). He then did three things: downloaded sexually oriented images, ordered a videotape (which was delivered by UPS), and sent an unsolicited child-porn video to the Thomases. This verification of the Thomas's activities led to a federal indictment on a dozen obscenity counts, mostly based on the downloaded images.

The couple was convicted of all but a child-pornography count based on the unsolicited video (which the jury probably viewed as entrapment). The Thomases now face a maximum sentence of five years in prison and a $250,000 fine on each of the charges. Their appeal, now pending, will likely be built around the claim that the jury instructions as to "community standards" were incorrect. (It's unclear in law whether Memphis, Tennessee, Milpitas, California, the Amateur Action BBS user base, or cyberspace in general is the community whose standards were breached.)

> "The real danger is the gradual erosion of individual liberties through the automation, integration, and inter-connection of many small, separate record-keeping systems, each of which alone may seem innocuous, even benevolent, and wholly justifiable."
>
> **U.S. PRIVACY PROTECTION STUDY COMMISSION, 1977**

The case raises the question of whether it makes sense to define "community standards" solely in terms of geographical communities. Now that an increasing number of Americans find themselves participating in "virtual communities" via the Internet, does it make sense to have what those citizens are allowed to bring into their own homes dictated by the arbitrary fact of where those homes happen to be?

Obscenity isn't protected by the First Amendment, but what qualifies as "obscenity" hasn't always been clear. After *Miller* v. *California,* a 1973 Supreme Court case, there has been no national standard as to what's obscene. In that case, the court stated that material is obscene (and therefore not protected by the First Amendment) if:

1. The average person, applying contemporary community standards, would find that the materials, taken as a whole, arouse immoral lustful desire (or, in the court's language, appeal to the "prurient interest").

2. The materials depict or describe, in a patently offensive way, sexual conduct specifically prohibited by applicable state law.

3. The work, taken as a whole, lacks serious literary, artistic, political, or scientific value.

To put it in lay terms, the trial court would ask questions something like these:

1. Is it designed to be sexually arousing?

2. Is it arousing in a way that one's local community would consider unhealthy or immoral?

3. Does it show acts whose depictions are specifically prohibited by state law?

4. Does the work, when taken as a whole, lack significant literary, artistic, scientific, or social value?

It's time for the courts to revisit the Miller obscenity standard. In the face of changes in communications media and the evolving nature of "community," the courts should modify the application of the Miller standard to prevent this kind of prosecutorial overreaching. Failing that, the courts should abandon the "community standards" approach altogether.

Until these issues are addressed, this case will create a chilling effect all over the country, as BBSs, Web sites, ISPs, individuals, and corporate Internet participants censor themselves or go offline in order to avoid prosecution. The case sends a frightening message to virtual communities: "It doesn't matter if you're abiding by your own community's standards; you have to abide by Memphis's as well."

It's the sensational cases that always seem to make headlines—headlines about children accessing porn or being abducted after being contacted over the Internet. In truth, though, these dangers probably exist only to the extent that they do on the streets of your town, where sexually oriented books and videos are available and child abductions do take place. Still, you would no more shut down your city because of an adult bookstore than you would lock your child up in the house to keep her safe. We teach our children to be cautious and aware of strangers, we instruct them on how to react when faced with a potential abduction, and we give them a healthy context for understanding sex and love as important aspects of human relations when we as parents determine that they're ready for this information.

If the prospect of your children happening upon questionable material is of concern to you, there are many software programs available that limit "accidental" exposure to particular kinds of material, to help you in your job of parenting.[2] Similar software can be used by any organization that has employees online and wants to remove the temptation for them to visit non–work-related Net sites on company time.

Just as there are restrictions on public access to sexually explicit paper-and-ink materials, so are there on the Net; and those who violate these restrictions are subject to serious punishment. The very same laws that protect us from "evildoers" in the real world also apply to those who use the Internet. In fact, the Internet is a useful tool for law enforcement agencies, helping officers to locate and apprehend just such offenders (as in the case of Kevin Mitnick, a much-publicized credit-card hacker whose escapades are addressed in Chapter 5). The point is that we don't need a new set of laws specifically for this medium; the ones we have are working well to protect us. What we do need (and are developing over time) is a set of community standards for cyberspace, much like the standards set by any *physical* community, to be respected and upheld by its citizens. We could use a little common sense and rational discourse too, to counteract the all-too-predictable sensationalistic news bites about these issues.

How Free Is *Your* Speech?

Are there limits you should be aware of as to what you can say online? There certainly are, and here common sense should be your guide. The freedom to say whatever you want must be tempered with personal (or organizational) responsibility. For example, the reason you can't yell "Fire!" in a crowded theater (when nothing is burning) is that the panic you could provoke is potentially dangerous, and the unnecessary damages that the theater could experience are potentially costly.

Certainly the same commonsense approach applies in cyberspace, where— as I've noted—the same laws that generally apply offline are enforced, including those against fraud, threats, bodily harm, harassment in the workplace, extortion, defamation, child pornography, obscenity, copyright violation, and trading in stolen credit-card numbers, to name a few. These laws are "medium-independent," meaning that they apply wherever such violations may be found.

If you choose to spread disinformation on the Net and an individual or business is harmed by your action, you may be found criminally or civilly liable, just as you would be anywhere else. The same principle holds for copyright infringement and any number of other issues that mirror our interactions in the physical world. (See the discussion of intellectual property in Chapter 4.) No one is anonymous on the Net. Unless you happen to have advanced computer-network knowledge, you leave a trail that a skilled investigator could trace you by every time you log on. The fact that your email address doesn't tell your real name or location doesn't mean you can't be found.

> "Just as the strength of the Internet is chaos, so the strength of our liberty depends upon the chaos and cacophony of the unfettered speech the First Amendment protects."
>
> **U.S. DISTRICT COURT JUSTICE DALZELL**
> (rendering his opinion in the overturning of the Communications Decency Act)

What can happen to you as punishment for irresponsible communication on the Net? Let's look at the case of Jake Baker, a student at the University of Michigan. He gained notoriety when the university suspended him without a hearing after he wrote a fictional story that appeared on a Usenet group (a publicly accessible bulletin board on the Net). Unfortunately for Mr. Baker, the story was a graphic depiction of rape, torture, and murder. He used his own account to post the article and used the name of a female student in one of his classes for the victim. Shortly after publication, Baker was arrested by the FBI and held without bond for twenty-nine days on the grounds that he was too dangerous to release. A more appropriate course of action for the school might have been to alert the victim to the possibility of civil legal action against Baker for defamation.

> "When the principal article of commerce (digital communication) looks so much like speech as to be indistinguishable from it, you'd better care about freedom of expression. In a global network environment, there's no difference between freedom of expression and freedom of enterprise."
>
> **JOHN PERRY BARLOW,**
> EFF co-founder

Apparently Baker, who had never been in trouble before (and had no intention of carrying out the acts described in his story), had touched a sensitive social nerve that the university president didn't hesitate to respond to. As it turns out, the university probably violated Baker's civil rights,[3] but in any case he suffered severe consequences. Even though he had never spoken to the student whose name he borrowed and had no intention of harming her, the result was disruption of his academic life and a monthlong incarceration.

The point here is that what you post on the Internet has definite impact, no matter how many or how few individuals are affected, even though the act of emailing or posting to the Net tends to make people feel rather insulated from potential consequences of their actions. Furthermore, the style of communication used on the Net is usually casual and conversational; and while that can be beneficial, it can also have serious consequences. Our words are easily retransmitted online, leaving an "impression" at every routing point along the network (more on this in the discussion on privacy in Chapter 3); and often words are taken, without question, as factual just because they're typed online. The potential for problems is enormous.

The key to avoiding these problems is to make each communication appropriate for its specific use. When emailing, remember that you're using a tool that's part telephone, part postal medium, part broadcasting. You might consider giving your email the "mom" test: if you wouldn't like your mom to see what you've written, consider rewriting it. And remember that email from a workplace or between employees is usually official correspondence and should be treated as such.

Of course, not everyone follows these guidelines. Some of what's emailed is highly offensive to those who receive it. What's the solution? How should inappropriate communication or the online availability of controversial material be handled? Is censorship the answer? Whether it's the Chinese government censoring dissidents, a religion wanting to silence nonbelievers, or those who deplore sexual content of any kind urging stricter obscenity standards, you can be assured that for anything controversial that's ever been published, there's someone out there who'd like to censor it.

The government of Hong Kong put controls on its local Internet users by raiding and confiscating the equipment of a number of independent Internet service providers (ISPs). Singapore does the job by running a national "proxy-server," which selects Web sites that it approves for its citizens to view—and limits people's access to *only* those. The Church of Scientology has been trying to silence its ideological adversaries with court actions against online critics *and* their service providers. In the United States, the fear that our children will access sexual material has been elevated out of proportion in the public consciousness. In response, Congress passed the Communications Decency Act (or CDA, later struck down as unconstitutional), which would have punished offenders with up to $250,000 in fines and two years in prison.[4]

We have a wonderful utility in the Internet that bears the promise of improving our lives and reaching out in ways we can't yet imagine to bring us closer together and achieve better understanding. The District Court judge who penned the decision striking down the CDA recognized this, saying, "Just as the strength of the Internet is chaos, so the strength of our liberty depends upon the chaos and cacophony of the unfettered speech the First Amendment protects."

The issues surrounding censorship of online communications are numerous and complex. Most stem from the question of jurisdiction, since the Net is the first truly global medium. Let's say your Web site or email message, which you created in your hometown of Toronto and resides on a server in Kuala Lumpur, is being read in Baghdad. Whose jurisdiction should determine whether it's appropriate legal communication? As in the Thomas BBS case cited earlier, a lot rests on which community's standards apply. There are no clear answers yet as to how such issues will be resolved, but for citizens and netizens, there's real cause for concern.

And what about extradition issues? Consider the example of the Dutch government, which apparently decided to investigate (or harass?) the xs4all.nl ISP at the behest of the German government—despite the fact that the offending material being transmitted via the

ISP was 100 percent legal in Holland. In most sorts of international extradition, the offense must be illegal in *both* jurisdictions. Should extradition be different for the Internet?

> "First they came for the hackers. But I never did anything illegal with my computer, so I didn't speak up. Then they came for the pornographers. But I thought there was too much smut on the Internet anyway, so I didn't speak up. Then they came for the anonymous remailers. But a lot of nasty stuff gets sent from anon.penet.fi, so I didn't speak up. Then they came for the encryption users. But I could never figure out how to work pgp[5] anyway, so I didn't speak up. Then they came for me. And by that time there was no one left to speak up."
>
> **ALARA ROGERS,**
> Aleph Press[6]

In the future, we're likely to see governments banding together to create new controlling bodies to deal with some of these global questions. If and when this happens, it's also probable that they'll be exercising control in an unprecedented way and with assumed authority. It's important for us, as individuals or representatives of an organization, to remember that governments derive their authority from us and should remain accountable to our will. Whether the new global community spreads democratic principles or repressive principles depends largely on how we respond to these challenges.

What we're seeing in the global response to free speech via the Net isn't encouraging. Whereas the U.S. approach is followed in many areas of international endeavor, few countries are eager to follow our lead in the determination to protect free speech. It's important, therefore, to research foreign restrictions that might apply to your Internet locality. (These are most likely available from your ISP.)

WEBLINKS TO THIS CHAPTER

TThomas BBS case:

http://www.eff.org/pub/Legal/Cases/AABBS_Thomases_Memphis

Jake Baker case:

http://www.eff.org/pub/Legal/Cases/Baker_UMich_case/

CDA:

http://www.eff.org/pub/Censorship/Internet_censorship_bills/

NOTES

1. The Internet was designed specifically with the capability to route around damaged nodes and connections so that it would still be a viable network in case of nuclear or other attack.

2. You can shop around for filtering software to limit access to certain Internet sites and newsgroups by checking out the following resources. This is an imperfect solution, however, because none of these programs can promise 100 percent accuracy in its filtering criteria. This lack of perfection has caused some to call these programs "censorware."

http://www.surfwatch.com/
http://www.cyberpatrol.com/
http://www.netnanny.com/

3. The federal charges against Baker based on the story he wrote were dropped, and Baker was then charged with transmitting threats across state lines in his email conversation about the story with a Canadian man. These charges were subsequently dismissed, with the judge finding email to be protected free speech. (It should be noted that workplace email isn't similarly protected. See the discussion on privacy in Chapter 3.)

For in-depth information on the Jake Baker case, visit *http://www.eff.org/pub/Legal/Cases/Baker_UMich_case/*.

4. The Communications Decency Act is important because it illustrates many of the issues surrounding censoring online communication. It was an amendment to the larger telecommunications reform bill passed by the U.S. Congress on February 1, 1996. It was ostensibly passed in response to the realization that a medium that comes into our homes and reaches our children with education and entertainment may also bring sexually explicit material. The reaction of our elected representatives was to do what they usually do in these circumstances: legislate!

Unfortunately, this legislation was written by individuals who were ignorant about that which they were attempting to regulate (sponsors: James Exon, D-Nebraska; and Dan

Coats, R-Indiana). Though the bill passed after less than forty-five minutes of debate—an unusually brief discussion for legislation that would seriously affect generations to come— it was found unconstitutional before it could be implemented (more on that later). An analysis of the bill shows the following:

- •It banned "indecent" material from most parts of the Internet without defining "indecent."
- •It failed to identify a means of regulation or enforcement.
- •It made that which is protected in print media subject to criminal sanctions in cyberspace.
- •It criminalized annoying messages that used harsh language, even if not obscene.
- •It specified penalties up to $250,000 and two years in prison for service providers that transmitted indecent material.

A last-minute addition to the bill prohibited open discussion of abortion and of many bodily functions in all but the most clinical of terms. Also prohibited were the seven dirty words made famous in a George Carlin monologue years ago. If this law were ever put into effect, we would see the chilling of free speech everywhere on the Net, along with censorship by service providers, many of which would simply go out of business. In addition, the law would give the FCC the same Internet jurisdiction they have over the broadcast media, further muddying enforcement and technical issues.

While making everything on the Net "safe" for children—as this law intended to do— would protect a segment of society, adults would be forced to sacrifice their own rights in the process. Had the legislators been aware of the alternatives to the CDA, they might have chosen to leave responsibility for children in homes with the parents, where we believe it belongs. (See our comments on filtering software in note 2, above).

As we noted, the bill sailed through Congress; it was then expeditiously signed by President Clinton. A coalition of rights organizations, including the ACLU and EFF, together with other individuals and organizations (including publishers, service providers, and educators), immediately filed suit with the U.S. District Court to block the law's implementation. The court issued an injunction to stay the law's enforcement until constitutionality could be reviewed. After that court found it unconstitutional, the U.S. Department of Justice appealed the decision, asking the highest court in the land to decide. The Supreme Court decision came down in July of 1996 in favor of protecting free speech on the Net.

5. PGP stands for "Pretty Good Privacy," a powerful encryption program for keeping communications private.

6. Based on a post–Nazi-Germany piece, to emphasize that the threat to personal liberty is exacerbated rather than eliminated when we turn our backs on such encroachment.

THREE PRIVACY, ANONYMITY, AND

SECURE COMMUNICATIONS[1]

Safeguarding Sensitive
Personal and Business Data
in the Information Age

"Privacy in one's associations ... may in many circumstances be indispensable to freedom of association, particularly where a group espouses dissident beliefs."

JOHN M. HARLAN, U.S. SUPREME COURT JUSTICE, 1958

"The real danger is the gradual erosion of individual liberties through the automation, integration, and interconnection of many small, separate record-keeping systems, each of which alone may seem innocuous, even benevolent, and wholly justifiable."

U.S. PRIVACY PROTECTION STUDY COMMISSION, 1977

Depending on where you live, you've probably come to expect a certain amount of privacy and anonymity in your life. For example, unless you're engaged in illegal or subversive activities, you don't expect that government agents will be peering into your home with high-tech surveillance equipment. You don't expect that your phone line will be tapped, or that when you send a letter to a friend or loved one it will be opened and read before it gets to the recipient.

Privacy and anonymity are so crucial to contemporary society that we could say there's a psychological need for them. In addition to serving that basic need, they help create a balance between the rights of individuals and the rights of organizations and governments. This kind of protection is important because of the unfair advantage organizations and governments have over individuals, based on their (usually) greater resources. The United States has the first government that's based on principles recognizing that people need to be protected *from* as well as *by* government. These principles have had immeasurable influence on many other societies in the modern free world, making their way into laws and customs around the globe that mirror (or even extend) our own.

Laws such as those that prohibit enforcement agencies from searching private premises without showing cause and obtaining a judicial warrant are among the effects of these principles visible today. Although originally crafted in response to King George's troops barging into colonists' homes and randomly seizing property, they've also been applied in law to keep snooping eyes and ears from your mail, your telephone calls, and other types of communications deemed to be "private."

Even though the world of electronic communication was beyond the imagination of most of our ancestors, the concepts and laws that were established for a free and open society are adequate to govern it if we give them a chance. Those laws were interpreted over the years to fit the new media as they developed; but now, with the electronic media developing faster than ever before, we've run aground. Unfortunately, the transition from the traditional media to the new interactive, electronic media isn't unfolding in a predictable way, which makes it difficult for common sense to govern the way we use and regulate these tools. The regulators (for example, members of the U.S. Congress) are woefully uneducated on the realities of how these media work and therefore don't know what protections and controls the new media should be afforded (based on existing precedents). That's why we have material banned from the Internet as "indecent" even though it's easily acquired at newsstands, and why citizens in California are being tried for crimes against the state of Tennessee when what they did was legal in California (see the discussion of the *Miller* case and *Thomas* case in Chapter 2).

What It Means to You

In the information age, potential abuses of access to private information about you could fill a book on their own. Consider the consequences of the "theft" of just a few bits of private information:

PRIVATE INFORMATION	ABUSE POTENTIAL
Your credit-card number	Fraudulent purchases
Your cellular phone ID	Fraudulent phone use
Your medical records	Insurance denial
	Rate abuse
Your computer password(s)	Misrepresentation in your name
	Theft of online time/privileges
	Illegal access to confidential files
	(and much more)

These items are representative of the kinds of information about you that are readily available to someone with the intent to steal from you, cheat you, or do you ill. Unfortunately, such a person is likely to get away with his or her wrongdoing, because it will have been done in your name. Cases of "identity theft"[2] and other ID-based fraud (such as the use of stolen credit cards) can wreak havoc on the lives of victims for years as they struggle to surmount the many bureaucratic barriers to correction of their records.

The same kinds of information and vulnerabilities exist with respect to your company's or organization's information too. Without encryption and authentication to protect confidential account and transaction information, commerce over public networks is conducted at great risk to the participants.

Indeed, the opportunities for damage via the new electronic media are staggering—opportunities for wrongful surveillance, abuse of information, erosion of protected rights, and a "dumbing down" of the public network that could cripple it. The good news is that we have technological tools at our fingertips to solve these problems, and we're making headway in legislative committees, the courts, corporate boardrooms, and standard-setting working groups toward formulating sensible policies to encourage rather than stifle future development. The path will be long and arduous, but less so for every individual citizen who makes it his or her business to become knowledgeable and get involved.

One of the main objectives of the Electronic Frontier Foundation is to educate citizens and legislators alike to the parallels between the new media and their predecessors, pointing out concerns regarding the issues of rights, responsibilities, and regulation, and posing possible solutions. There are no easy answers, to be sure—especially in the area of privacy, since privacy rights collide directly with other equally valuable rights, such as freedom of speech and public access to government information. It's our hope that this chapter will expand your understanding regarding these complex personal and organizational issues and that our suggestions will offer you a course of action to facilitate your personal and/or organizational goals.

Privacy in Cyberspace

Whether you get online via an online service such as CompuServe or America Online (AOL), a commercial access provider or Internet service provider (ISP), or an electronic bulletin-board service (BBS), you have pretty much the same types of communications options available to you. These options include email, bulletin-board or newsgroup postings, live "chat" areas, and Web sites. Any of these applications can utilize the Internet, which is actually a global network linking smaller individual computer networks (such as that of the service provider you subscribe to).

> "Relying on the government to protect your privacy is like asking a peeping tom to install your window blinds."
>
> **JOHN PERRY BARLOW,**
> EFF co-founder

Information sent over this vast network may pass through dozens of different computer systems on the way to its destination. Typically, each of the systems—or nodes on the network—has its own operator (sysop) and/or system administrator (sysadmin). These other networks relay the data you send to its ultimate destination, and in the process may be capable of capturing and retrieving your messages or other data. You can see, then, how your own ISP, or another provider that you aren't even aware of, could acquire your personal communications.

The level of privacy you can expect from an online activity is to some extent dictated by the nature of that activity: a note posted on a bulletin board, for example, is obviously less private than a note emailed to a single recipient. Sometimes, however, an activity that *appears* to be private is not. The safest assumption is that there's no absolute right or expectation of privacy online.

What You Need to Know About "Public" Areas

Many online areas and activities are open to public inspection. A person browsing in these areas and engaging in these activities should have no expectation of privacy. In fact, according to federal law, it isn't illegal for anyone to view or disclose an electronic communication if the communication is "readily accessible" to the public.

For example, a message you post to a public newsgroup or forum is available for anyone to view, copy, and store. In addition, details such as your name, email address, and information about your service provider are usually available for inspection as part of the message itself. Furthermore, most public postings made on the Internet are archived in searchable databases. These public messages can therefore be accessed by anyone at anytime—even years after the message was originally written.

Other activities, while public, are open to a narrower audience, allowing your message to be sent to multiple but specific recipients. Online newsletters, for example, are usually sent to a mailing list of subscribers. These lists, sometimes known as "listservers," enable individual readers to publish comments directly to the entire circulation. When you reply to email that you received via a "listserver," you should take care to see that the reply is addressed only to the individual who sent the original message. Otherwise, your reply will go to the entire list.

Make sure that an individual—for example, "sysop@vocetalk.com"—

is in your TO field when you reply to listserver mail, unless you want the entire subscriber base to see your message.

You shouldn't expect that your service account information will be kept private, though policies regarding revealing your identity and allowing access to information about you vary radically from provider to provider. Responsible Internet service providers adhere to a policy of informed consent—in other words, you're informed of their policies before signing up and given the opportunity to opt in or out of a particular offering.

Some service providers sell their membership lists to direct marketers without the members' knowledge or consent. Most provide online "member directories" that publicly list all subscribers and may include additional personal information, such as real names, telephone numbers and addresses. Even individuals with direct Internet accounts can be identified with the help of "finger" technology, which lets a knowledgeable user find out who else is online and gather personal data about those people. Most service providers will allow users to have their information removed from member directories upon request, however, and some won't accept finger queries.

For more information on the subject of ISPs and privacy, see the discussion on junk email in Chapter 5.

What You Need to Know About "Semi-Private" Areas

Often the presence of security or access safeguards on certain forums or services leads users to believe that communications made within these areas are private. For example, some bulletin-board services maintain forums that are restricted to users who have a password. While communications made in these forums may initially be read only by the members with access, there's nothing to prevent those members from recording the communications and later transmitting them elsewhere.

One example of this kind of activity is the real-time "chat" conference, in which participants type live messages directly to the computer screens of other participants. Although these activities are often described as private by the service provider, chat-line users can capture, store, and transmit these communications to others outside the chat service. Additionally, these activities are subject to the same monitoring exceptions that apply to "private" email (see below).

What You Need to Know About "Private" Areas

Unlike postal mail, email isn't really private. Regardless of what your service provider's policy is with respect to "personal" correspondence, it's important to note the many reasons why email messages can't be considered private unless they're encrypted or otherwise made unreadable to prying eyes.[3] This lack of privacy is due to the architecture of the Net (and of digital communications in general), which requires there to be a copy of your message on the machine that generated it (your computer), the machine that receives it (your recipient's computer), and every routing point along the way between the two. (This architecture will be explained in greater detail in discussions on email security and email in the workplace later in this chapter.)

Recognizing that electronic communications deserve the same kinds of privacy protection that traditional media are afforded, various governments have put some protections in place. The U.S. Electronic Communications Privacy Act (ECPA, 1986, 18USC2516), for example, prohibits the reading or disclosure of the contents of an electronic communication not intended for him or her. This law, which applies to telephone or email messages, is somewhat outdated, as are many similar statutes in other parts of the world.

You should be aware of the following significant exceptions to the ECPA, however:

1. Your service provider can view and/or disclose private communications if either of the involved parties consents. This consent is sometimes accomplished via the small print in a written agreement required for new members at registration.

2. If communication is conducted from a place of business or on an employer's network, that employer has the right to access and inspect its contents.

3. A service provider, given reason to suspect that a sender is attempting to damage the system or harm another user, can view private email. There must be some justification, however; random monitoring isn't permitted.

If a system operator intercepts your mail for any lawful reason, he or she isn't allowed to disclose the contents to anyone other than the person to whom it was addressed. There are a few exceptions, however. The sysop can disclose a message to law enforcement officials investigating a crime, for example, but only after obtaining a court-ordered search warrant. Details of who can apply for a warrant, and how and when the application should be handled, are set forth in the ECPA. Additionally, the sysop can disclose a message if another party to the message consents to that disclosure to a specified individual.

If unlawful disclosure to an unauthorized person takes place, a sysop isn't in violation of the ECPA if he or she can prove that the disclosure was made accidentally. (In that case, the sysop may be liable for damages due to negligence, however.)

If a message that you had intended to be private becomes public, remember that another party to that message may have given consent for disclosure of its contents, permitting any sysop along its path to view it legally. You need to make sure of the circumstances before you take action against anyone.

Browsing Web Sites

Do online services track and record user activities? They certainly *can,* and evidently in some cases they do so.

Internet users can retrieve information or documents from sites on the World Wide Web (www) and from FTP sites ("FTP" stands for File Transfer Protocol, and represents a storage site from which you can download, or in some cases upload, files via the Internet. In the early days of the Internet, you needed a program designed specifically for FTP to access these files. Today, many such archives are accessible through Web browsers). They can also simply "browse" these services without any additional interaction. Many users expect that such activities—especially browsing—are anonymous, but there's absolutely no guarantee of that. It's possible to record many online activities, including which newsgroups or files a subscriber has accessed and which Web sites a subscriber has visited. This information can be collected both by a subscriber's own service provider and by the sysops of remote sites that a subscriber has visited.

Some Web-browsing programs create files called "cookies," which are left on your computer's hard drive after visiting certain Web sites. These cookies, which are used by the browser to store data about your visit to the Web site, then communicate with that Web site's server the next time you visit. They can be time-savers if you belong to sites that require membership or a password to access them, but they also harbor the potential for reducing your privacy online. Marketers have found cookies useful as targeting tools for sending junk email or for displaying banner-ads designed to appeal to you, personally, when you visit a site. Such marketers often work with many Web sites at once to share cookies between them. Though this is most often done simply to prevent you from receiving the same ad over and over again, far less cheerful practices are enabled by such collusion, which may go on without the user's control, consent, or even awareness.

Wanna Cookie?

In World Wide Web parlance, a cookie is a file generated by your browser in response to a request from the Web site you're visiting—a request that also tells your computer what information to record. That cookie then stays on your computer and is referenced when you visit that site again later. Not all Web sites generate these files, but those that do usually use the information for things like remembering passwords (if they're required at the site), remembering what you've already seen at the site, and perhaps recording purchases made there. Most browsers give you the option of changing your settings so that you can be notified of a cookie request before it's responded to; then you can either manually or automatically accept or reject the cookie. If you reject a cookie, however, you may be unable to access that site.

What you do while visiting various Web sites—sometimes called the "clickstream" or "transaction-generated" information—is of great value to marketers and may be a lucrative source of revenue for service providers or site operators. For example, your selection of products, how long you viewed the pages, and where you went within a site can tell a lot about your likes and dislikes. These browsing patterns may help create a profile that marketers later use to target sales messages to you. If you happen to visit sites that have sensitive or controversial content, you may not want that information being used as described here.

There are steps you can take to protect yourself from information transmitted by these cookies, including software filters from companies such as Pretty Good Privacy, Inc., WebFilter, and Junkbusters.[4] Junkbuster, from the latter firm, is a freely distributed product designed to eliminate ads and cookies by routing users' Web sessions through a filter at the ISP level or on another machine, called a "proxy server."

Because the practice of collecting browsing patterns is becoming more prevalent, online users should be aware that it poses a significant threat to online privacy. It's a good idea to contact your service provider and ask whether this type of information is collected on their system. Additionally, online users should educate themselves about what information is transmitted to remote computers by the software that they use to browse remote sites. Most World Wide Web browsers invisibly provide Web site operators with information about a user's service provider and about other Web sites that user has visited. Most Web browsers are programmed to transmit a user's email address to each Web site he or she visits, along with the address of the site that provided the hyperlink—all without the user's knowledge.

Users who access the Internet from work should know that employers, too, are increasingly monitoring the Internet sites that each employee visits. This is totally within their rights, just as it's totally within *yours* to be aware of your company's policy. We urge you to inquire about your employer's online usage and privacy policy. If there is none, you might recommend that such a policy be developed.

Like messages sent online, subscriber transaction records are accessible to law enforcement officials, but again the officials must obtain a court order demonstrating that the records are relevant to an ongoing criminal investigation. This provision prevents "fishing expeditions" by government officials hoping to find evidence of crimes by accident.

Protecting Your Hard Drive

Be aware that service providers can access information stored in your computer without your knowledge. Many of the commercial online services automatically download graphics and program upgrades to the user's home computer. Recent news reports claim that certain online services have admitted to both accidental and intentional "prying" into the memory of home computers whose owners have signed on with them. If those reports prove true, it's possible that personal files could have been copied and collected by the online services.

Because it's difficult to detect hard-drive intrusions, online users should be aware of this potential privacy abuse and investigate new services thoroughly before signing on. Always ask for the privacy policy of any online service you intend to use, and look for privacy statements at Web sites you visit.

In addition to the possibility of intrusion by an online service's access software, new Web technologies (such as Java and ActiveX) allow for the inclusion in Web pages of miniature applications—known as "applets"—that run on the visiting user's own machine, and these may pose a variety of security and privacy risks. The developers of these Web applications are working hard to resolve such issues, but it's not clear that total protection from these potential intruders is possible.

The Flap over Encryption

Encryption is a method of scrambling an email message or file so it appears as gibberish to anyone who doesn't know how to unscramble it. The privacy advantage of encryption is that anything encrypted is virtually inaccessible to anyone other than the designated recipient. Thus private information can be encrypted, transmitted, and then stored or distributed without fear that it will be scrutinized by outsiders. With the use of encryption strictly regulated, decisions being considered now in legislatures and courtrooms will affect everyone who uses the public networks, along with anyone who has a computer file containing confidential medical or tax records, or love letters or other writings—in other words, virtually everyone.

> "One if by land, two if by sea."
> **PAUL REVERE**,
> civilian encryption user, 1775

The benefits of this technology to those wishing to maintain their privacy are evident; however, there are less obvious benefits as well. For example, the very same algorithm that prevents outsiders from reading an encrypted email message is capable of establishing an unimpeachable identification of who sent that message. This identification feature is ideal for protecting financial transactions online. No one besides the parties involved in the transaction can tell who's buying or selling, what's changing hands, and for how much. In addition, all details about the accounts being accessed—numbers, passwords, and balances, for example—remain private, and the parties involved are certain of whom they're dealing with.

A common form of encryption, called "public key cryptography," is a simple, elegant solution to offering autonomous security—that is, security where users aren't dependent on the trust of a third party to ensure privacy. Here's how it works:

Each user in the system has two closely related keys, one public and one private. The public key is distributed by the user via email, on a Web page, or wherever is deemed appropriate. It looks something like this:

——BEGIN PUBLIC KEY BLOCK——

mQCPAzMSAEoAAAEEAOVznrQT9r8gBHUQHk+ozXY0heAuWLOsPj4Ypp8rqBi35F8A

BgYJSovQUi7bpC3fHv53FQab1NJg3YrHd7c/HSGrXuZ2PKZG/Uet+lLxiWVmZyst

Qa64+yQXiLиuQXbktX07a3cePBMjyjw6lsQEAmJ3pKrg35fhwq0DsKxJKxudABEB

AAG0G1JCR2VsbWFuPGN5YmVyZ3V5QHdlbGwuY29tPg==

=4zGm

——END PUBLIC KEY BLOCK——

The private key is kept tightly secret, accessible only by the owner of that key. Using an application such as Pretty Good Privacy, a message encoded with the public key can be decoded only by the recipient's private key. So if you wanted to send a private message, you'd encode the message with the recipient's public key. (The message would look very much like the public key itself.) To decode it, the recipient would use his or her private key. To reply back to you, the recipient would use the same process, encoding his or her message with *your* public key. Upon receipt, you would then decode it with your private key.

The same principle also provides for digital "signatures," allowing a message to travel unencrypted while the author's signature is encrypted. The public key system then enables you to verify both that the alleged author is in fact the person who sent you the message and that the message wasn't modified in transit.

A Brief History of Encryption

Unfortunately, if you use the strongest, most efficient level of cryptography in communications that cross the U.S. border (either as a final destination or en route via Internet digressions), you're committing a serious federal crime as a dealer in arms! Cryptography software is classified as a "munition" by the U.S. government (and some others, such as the administrations of Canada and Japan), and those who "export" it are subject to serious penalties as stipulated in the International Traffic in Arms Regulations (ITAR, 22 CFR 120.1 *et seq.*).[5] However, the use of cryptography *within* the United States isn't currently restricted, at least not for U.S. citizens. To understand why this situation exists, it's necessary to go back to pre–World War II days to see how sophisticated mechanical encryption came into use.

Prior to and during the Cold War, encryption was a very effective method of protecting national security. Not only did it prevent foreign governments from accessing classified military communications; it also, because of U.S. technological superiority, enabled "cracking" the encrypted messages of hostile nations. Thus cryptography became a tool that enabled U.S. intelligence to maintain its global advantage.

With the advent of the personal computer, secure information transmission became an issue relevant to businesses and individuals as well as governments. In 1975, a young computer wizard named Whitfield Diffie developed a system called public key cryptography—the system described above. This method of splitting and transmitting the encoding-decoding tools helped bring the power of encryption technology to computer users outside the government for the first time.

As the Cold War began to wind down, the government continued to enforce restrictions on the export of military technologies—despite the fact that those technologies, as products in mass-market commerce, were no longer the purview of the military. U.S. businesses were among the first to register their displeasure at these outdated laws governing encryption technology. Not only did these laws hamper the ability of businesses to develop online commerce, they also prohibited (and still prohibit) the entire software industry in the United States from competing in the global marketplace. Companies that produce applications such as spreadsheets, terminal programs,

Web browsers, word processors, email suites, and databases need to be able to build security into their products. Instead of maintaining a significant advantage in the technology and marketing of software products with cryptographic security features, U.S. companies were/are forced to either develop different products for export and domestic use (a cost-prohibitive requirement) or to simply not offer strong crypto products at all. Meanwhile, other nations, such as the Netherlands, have jumped in to fill the global market void with their own products.

With the end of the Cold War, the U.S. government turned to domestic crime and terrorism as its justification for prohibitions on cryptography. In 1991, an activist-programmer by the name of Phil Zimmerman announced completion of a product he'd been working on in his spare time. His program, called Pretty Good Privacy (PGP), implemented some public-domain algorithms in a way that allowed nonprogrammers to easily use it. Zimmerman had been hearing rumors from Washington hinting that strong cryptography (over 40-bit strength) might soon be outlawed altogether, so he felt that he needed to act quickly. Although he'd originally planned to offer PGP as a for-profit product, he recognized the importance of having this tool in the hands of as many people as possible, in as many places as possible, so he decided to distribute it for free. By giving it to friends who subsequently posted it for download from the Internet, he made strong cryptography available to the entire world practically overnight.[6]

Almost as swiftly, he was informed that he was the subject of an FBI investigation for "illegally trafficking in arms." That investigation continued for over five years, making life difficult and costly for the independent programmer, who had simply acted on his belief that we all have the right to private communication. In distributing PGP, he was giving users of the Net the electronic equivalent of an envelope in which to place their private letters.

Enter the Clipper Chip

In 1993, the Clinton administration demonstrated that the rumors Zimmerman had heard were probably true. The White House, at the urging of the National Security Agency (NSA), introduced the "Clipper Chip" initiative as its "solution" to the online security problem. After three revised proposals, each meeting with harsh criticism from Internet and civil liberties groups, the Clipper appears to have been scrapped. Had it been implemented, this proposal would have created far more problems than it could have hoped to solve.

In a nutshell, the government was proposing that all computers be manufactured with a U.S. government–designed hardware encryption system installed (dubbed "Skipjack"), which allows a certain level of encryption, and required that all users subscribe to a "key escrow" authority (ostensibly a government agency) to hold their decoding key. Thus, users must trust that this key escrow agency will serve their interests in all cases. This would be like giving a copy of your house key to the local office of the FBI "in case" they needed to get in. This was another example of government using the threat of crime and terrorism as the justification for wanting to retain control of your private information.

This proposal was met with extreme criticism from Internet and civil liberties groups from all parts of the globe on various grounds, such as:

- doubts as to whether a key escrow system would actually produce the desired law enforcement results

- the level of strength and integrity of the algorithm and the security of the key escrow system itself

- the advisability of a government-developed and classified algorithm

- its practicality and commercial acceptability

- the effect of the proposal on U.S. competitiveness and the balance of trade

- possible implications for the development of digital communications

- the effect on the right to privacy and other constitutional rights.

Leading a coalition of organizations speaking in defense of those rights, EFF published its official policy on this issue based on these principles:

I. Private access to cryptography must be unhindered.
   A. *There must be no laws restricting domestic use of cryptography.*
   B. *There must be no restrictions on the export of products, services, or information because they contain cryptographic algorithms.*

II. Cryptography policy and technical standards must be set in open, public forums.
   A. *All participants in the policy debate on these issues, particularly law enforcement and national security agencies, must submit their arguments to public scrutiny.*
   B. *Any civilian encryption standard must be published and exposed to rigorous public challenge.*

III. Encryption must become a part of the information infrastructure to provide security, to protect privacy, and to give each individual control over his or her own identity.
   A. *Each user must be free to choose whether or not to use key escrow, and to specify who (if anyone) should have copies of their keys.*

B. *Government at all levels should explore cryptography's potential to replace identity-based or dossier-based systems, such as driver's licenses, credit cards, checks, and passports, with less invasive technology.*

IV. New technologies must not erode constitutional protections—particularly the right to speak, publish, and assemble, and to be free from unreasonable searches and seizures.

A. *There must be no broadening of governmental access to private communications and records, through wiretap law or otherwise, unless there's a public consensus that the risks to safety outweigh the risks to liberty and that our safety will actually be increased by the broadened access.*

We recognize that the combination of digital communications and encryption technology does indeed threaten some of law enforcement's current investigative techniques. We also recognize that encryption will actually *prevent* many of the online crimes that are likely to occur without it. We further believe that these technologies will create new investigative tools for law enforcement, even as they make old ones obsolete. Entering this new environment, private industry, law enforcement, and private citizens must work together to balance the requirements of both liberty and security. But technology halts for no one, not even the law.

Encryption and the Courts:
Bernstein v. *U.S. Dept. of State*

In February 1995, EFF sponsored a civil court action designed to have the unconstitutionality of the State Department's policies reviewed and overturned. In *Bernstein* v. *U.S. Department of State*, a Berkeley,

California, mathematician sued, challenging both the government's designation of encryption software as a "munition" and its policy of subjecting such software to extensive export controls. According to then-current law, distributing data or encryption software without government approval was (under certain circumstances) a criminal act punishable by ten years in prison and fines of a million dollars or more.

> **"**In order for the information superhighway to reach its full potential, network security must be assured. Kevin Mitnick, who stole users' passwords as they logged on and used those passwords to break into computers across the network, could have been stopped with encryption. If the passwords, credit-card numbers, and long-distance toll access codes he stole had been encrypted, he would not have been able to make use of the information he had obtained. But current U.S. encryption policy makes the deployment of good security a criminal offense.... [Current policy] refuses to accept that "the cat is out of the bag."
>
> **SHARI STEELE,**
> EFF counsel (comments excerpted from testimony before the Committee to Study National Cryptography Policy of the National Research Council, April 1995)

Daniel Bernstein, then a Ph.D. candidate at the University of California, was told that he'd have to register as an arms dealer under the International Traffic in Arms Regulations (ITAR) if he wanted to publish an encryption program he'd developed. (These regulations prevent individuals from engaging in otherwise legal communications when the subject is encryption.) Bernstein applied for the appropriate permission to publish both his program and a paper describing how the software works.

The lawsuit challenged the export-control scheme as an "impermissible prior restraint on speech, in violation of the First

Amendment." Software and its associated documentation, the plaintiff contended, are *published,* not *manufactured;* they're constitutionally protected works of communication, like a movie, a book, or a telephone conversation. These communications can't be suppressed by the government except under very narrow conditions—conditions that aren't met by the vague and overbroad export-control laws. In denying people the right to publish such information freely, these laws, regulations, and procedures unconstitutionally abridge the right to speak, to publish, to associate with others, and to engage in academic inquiry and study. They also have the effect of restricting the availability of a means for individuals to protect their privacy, which is also a constitutionally protected interest.

More specifically, the current export-control process:

• Allows bureaucrats to restrict publication without ever going to court

• Provides too few procedural safeguards for First Amendment rights

• Requires publishers to register with the government, creating (in effect) a "licensed press"

• Disallows general publication by requiring recipients to be individually identified

• Is sufficiently vague that ordinary people can't know what conduct is allowed and what conduct is prohibited

• Is overbroad because it prohibits conduct that's clearly protected (such as speaking to foreigners within the United States)

• Is overbroad because it prohibits export of certain software that contains no cryptography on the theory that cryptography could be added to it later

- Egregiously violates the First Amendment by prohibiting private speech on cryptography because the government wishes its own opinions on cryptography to guide the public instead

- Exceeds the authority granted by Congress in the export-control laws in many ways, as well as exceeding the authority granted by the Constitution

If ultimately successful in its challenge of the export-control laws, this suit will clear the way for cryptographic software to be treated like any other kind of software. This will allow companies such as Microsoft, Apple, IBM, and Sun to build high-quality security and privacy protection into their operating systems. Although they can do so now for the domestic market, they're currently crippled in the increasingly important global market for secure software and online transactions. If this suit is successful, it will also allow computer and network users, including those who use the Internet, much more freedom to build and exchange their own cryptography solutions—solutions like the PGP encryption program. And it will enable the next generation of Internet protocols to come with built-in cryptographic security and privacy, addressing a major weakness of today's Internet infrastructure.

So *will* the suit be successful? It's hard to tell. Bernstein won the first round, but the government has appealed the District Court ruling. Furthermore, the White House, in an attempt to evade the impact of this case, managed to have the jurisdiction switched from the State Department's Office of Defense Trade Controls to the Commerce Department in early 1997.

". . . For the purposes of First Amendment analysis, this court finds that source code is speech." This precedent, set in the preliminary *Bernstein* decision in December of 1996 by Federal Judge Marilyn Hall Patel, is incredibly important. Judge Patel concluded that the Arms Export Control Act is a prior restraint on speech because it

required Bernstein to apply for and obtain a license from the government to publish his ideas. Using the Pentagon Papers case as precedent, she ruled that the government's "interest of national security alone does not justify a prior restraint."

Judge Patel also held that the government's required licensing procedure fails to provide adequate procedural safeguards. When the government acts via laws and regulations to suppress protected speech, it must reduce the chance of illegal censorship by the bureaucrats involved. Pending the appeal, Professor Bernstein is free to publish his ideas without asking the government's permission first.

Judge Patel also ruled that the export controls restrict material based solely on the content, not for any other reason. "Category XIII(b) is directed very specifically at applied scientific research and speech on the topic of encryption." The government had argued that it restricts because of the material's *function,* not its content.

Furthermore, the judge found the arms regulations dangerously vague: the ITAR doesn't adequately define how information that's available to the public "through fundamental research in science and engineering" is exempt from the export restrictions. "This subsection . . . does not give people . . . a reasonable opportunity to know what is prohibited." The failure to precisely define what objects and actions are regulated creates confusion and a chilling effect.

That chilling effect is evidenced in the fact that Bernstein was unable to publish his encryption algorithm for over four years. Many other cryptographers and ordinary programmers have also been restrained from publishing because of the vagueness of the ITAR. Brian Behlendorf, a maintainer of the popular public-domain Apache Web server program, notes that "no cryptographic source code was ever distributed by the Apache project. Despite this, the Apache server code was deemed by the NSA to violate the ITAR." Judge Patel also adopted a narrower definition of the term "defense article" in order to save it from unconstitutional vagueness.

The immediate effect of this decision is that Bernstein is now free to teach his cryptography class in his usual way. He can post his class materials on the Internet and discuss upcoming class materials with other professors without being held in violation of the ITAR. "I'm very pleased," Bernstein said in a press release. "Now I won't have to tell my students to burn their notebooks."

It's unclear exactly where Judge Patel's decision applies, however— in the Northern District of California only, an area encompassing San Francisco and Silicon Valley, or throughout the country. Check with your own lawyer if you contemplate taking action based on the decision.

And there's further ambiguity. It isn't yet clear from Judge Patel's decision whether the export controls on "object code" (the executable form of computer programs that source code is automatically trans- lated into) have been overturned. It may be that existing export con- trols will continue to apply to runnable software products, such as Netscape's browser, until another court case challenges that part of the restrictions.

Lead attorney on the *Bernstein* case is Cindy Cohn, of McGlashan and Sarrail in San Mateo, California, who has rendered her services pro bono. Major assistance has been provided by Shari Steele of the EFF staff; John Gilmore, EFF board member; and Lee Tien, counsel to John Gilmore.

Full text of the lawsuit and other paperwork filed in the case is available from EFF's online archives. The exhibits that contain crypto- graphic information aren't available online, however, because making them publicly available on the Internet could be considered an illegal export until the law is struck down! The noncryptographic exhibits and other documents, including the complaint and a series of letters between Bernstein and various government people regarding crypto export, are available at *http://www.eff.org/pub/Privacy/ITAR_export/ Bernstein_case.*

Like freedom of speech, privacy issues vary widely from culture to culture. In the few cases that have been brought to court in this country, encryption technology has been determined to be equivalent to protected speech. Still, there's a strong law enforcement lobby in the United States seeking to prohibit the export of that technology—despite the fact that the same technology is already available all over the world.

Safeguards for Intellectual Property

Encryption is a form of protection for an individual or organization's privacy. When it comes to intellectual property—songs, writings (including software), art, photography, and so on—ownership and compensation are serious concerns. One solution to provide payment to creators is a system that manages these micro-transactions (transactions too small to warrant having a person supervise each one individually). This will require strong security and a means of exchanging money in a way that doesn't lend itself to fraud. One such method is the use of a third-party system (such as Cyber-Cash) that mediates transactions between browsers and Web sites. Another system soon to debut is the "Smart-Card." Smart-Cards have a memory chip in them that will keep track of a user's account information. Card readers will attach to home and public computers to allow Net access and to authenticate user identification, not to mention fees for various services and intellectual property.

The good news is that technologies capable of doing just that are available today. The bad news is that they come at a price: by adding micro-costs to every act of reading or writing on the Net, they'll drive user costs up rapidly. Technologies such as "digital watermark," for example, are designed to prevent piracy of works purchased online or through other digital media. Though still relatively new and not widely used, they show great promise, because they can be customized to provide user-identity tracking or other limited information whenever a file is transmitted.

Supplementing Encryption: Anonymous Remailers

Because it's relatively easy to determine the name and email address of anyone who posts a message on the Net or sends email, the practice of using anonymous remailing programs—available through anonymous servers on the Internet—is becoming increasingly common. These programs receive email, strip off all identifying information, then forward the mail to the appropriate address. Some remailers allow the process in reverse as well; by assigning numeric pseudonymous addresses and maintaining a database matching pseudonyms with real addresses, they permit replies. This type of remailer has been the subject of attempts to force disclosure, via subpoenas and other legal actions, of the real identity of users. (Cases in point revolve around messages hostile to the Church of Scientology and to the nation of Singapore, in separate incidents.)

The use of anonymous remailers is legitimate and responsible if the information communicated is controversial or dangerous to the sender's safety (or the safety of others), as with political dissidents; other legitimate uses include "whistleblowing," discussing sensitive topics (in an online AIDS support group, for example), or providing truly anonymous tips to journalists. There are several anonymous servers available on the Internet. A list of the active ones, along with performance comparisons and information on their use, is available at *http://www.cs.berkeley.edu/-raph/remailer-list.html.*

Some people are concerned that anonymous remailers are too subject to abuse. While it's true that they can be misused for making threats or slandering with impunity, our society has long recognized that the value of having anonymity available greatly outweighs the risks of its abuse. And we have historical precedents to support that belief—from the pseudonymous Federalist Papers and centuries of anonymous political pamphleteering to contemporary and very widespread implementations of anonymous systems, such as paper cash and pay phones.

Medical Privacy

With the unique sensitivity of personal medical information and the ability of digital media to distribute that information easily, the topic of medical privacy is of special concern to consumers online. At first glance, medical records appear to be one of the few truly confidential areas in our lives. Various laws, combined with the long-standing doctor-patient privilege, would seem to make it all but impossible for others to gain access to medical records. But the laws contain exemptions, and patients usually must waive their right to confidentiality in return for insurance coverage. The fact is that you probably have a false sense of security.

This situation is intensified by the digitization of information and its availability over public networks. There are many ways in which this personal information about you can be abused, only some of which fall within the scope of the electronic frontier. The latest consumer and professional information related to medical data security can be obtained by contacting this organization:

American Health Information Management Association
919 North Michigan Avenue
Suite 1400
Chicago, IL 60611
(312) 787-2672
http://www.ahima.org

Whenever you receive treatment or consultation from a health professional, a record of that interaction is created. Traditionally, these records have been tucked in files kept in the office of the medical service provider and made available only to the patient, to others specified by the patient (such as the insurance company) with the patient's written permission (via either a blanket waiver or a consent form), or to law enforcement personnel (in response to a court-ordered subpoena). And we as a society have valued that perceived privacy. Given the sensitive nature of medical records, there are countless justifiable reasons why someone might not want them made available without prior knowledge or permission. Such records contain information that reveals details about a person's lifestyle—mention of a sexually transmitted disease may suggest multiple sexual partners, for example, while lung cancer may suggest smoking—and about family medical history.

The debate over the future of medical record-keeping includes the possibility that one day doctors won't keep their own records; instead, a single file with an individual's complete medical history will be stored in a regional or national database. Some say this will make the system more efficient, helping people keep track of personal information and allowing them to monitor records for mistakes. Privacy advocates, however, are concerned about possible secondary uses of this medical information, as well as unnecessary employer access and other unauthorized access.

Medical privacy is also threatened by the public nature of certain phone and fax communication. You might want to find out if your health-care provider has a policy on use of cordless and cellular phones and fax machines to discuss and transmit medical information. (A more thorough discussion of cordless and cellular phones appears later in this chapter.)

There's a general consensus among private citizens and health-care professionals that addressing the confidentiality of health records is of vital importance in the continuing evolution of the health-care system. These issues are currently being debated by federal and state policymakers. If you have an opinion or concern in this area, contact your legislators (listed at *http://www.congress.org*).

Privacy in the Workplace

If you're an employer or employee of a company or institution, you've probably wondered from time to time just how private your communications from and within the workplace are. If you happen to be the employer, you've probably had to consider just what level of communications supervision makes sense, based on the needs of your business, the type of personnel you employ, and so on. While there are laws governing the monitoring of activities in the workplace, they vary widely from state to state in the United States and range even more widely in other countries.

The general rule regarding privacy in the workplace is that there is none. That's an exaggeration, of course, but it's probably better to be cautious in this regard than endanger your livelihood or that of others. This advice grows out of the knowledge that there's a basic conflict of interests between employers and their employees: *employers want to be sure that their employees are doing a good job, but employees don't want their every sneeze or trip to the watercooler logged.*

New technologies make it possible for employers to monitor many aspects of their employees' jobs, especially those aspects that involve telephones, computer terminals, and email and voicemail. With few exceptions, such monitoring is virtually unregulated. Unless company policy specifically states otherwise, your employer can listen to, watch, and read most of your workplace communications. Even where there are laws to the contrary, there's very little enforcement of them to deter unscrupulous behavior.

Telephone Monitoring

The telephone is generally outside the scope of this book's focus (new media); however, the principles and laws that apply to the phone often govern the new electronic media as well. Therefore, we'll include information about phone use in the workplace as a point of reference for email, voicemail, and other tools.

In most instances, employers have the right to listen to employee telephone calls. They can, for example, monitor calls with clients or customers for reasons of quality control. Some states and other jurisdictions make very particular, and sometimes counterintuitive, exceptions and special rules regarding phone use. For example, in California, when the parties to a call are all within the state—but *only* then—the law requires that they be informed (via a beep tone on the line or a recorded message) that the conversation is being recorded or monitored. However, because not every business is aware of this requirement, some in-state calls are still monitored without warning.

There's a gray area in the law regarding personal calls. What case law has concluded is that an employer must cease monitoring a call as soon as he or she determines that said call is "personal." Of course, if the company's stated policy prohibits personal calls, employees risk being monitored as to the existence of such calls (even if the content of those calls is unassailable).

The best way to ensure the privacy of personal calls made at work is to use a pay phone or a separate phone designated by your employer for personal calls.

Headsets. If you wear a headset in the performance of your job, the conversations you have with co-workers are subject to monitoring by your employer in the same way that your conversations with clients or customers are. If you wear a headset, you should use the same care with co-workers that you'd use if you were talking to a customer or client on the phone. Some headsets have MUTE buttons that allow you to turn off the transmitter when you're not using the phone. Push it!

Telephone Records. If you're employed in a position that relies heavily on the telephone, you should know about a device called a "pen register." The pen register records each of the numbers called from specific extensions on a business telephone system and tells the employer how long each call lasted. This tool is often used for the legitimate purpose of determining an employee's performance, based on time spent calling customers, but it can also be used to determine if personal or non–business-related calls have been made.

Computer Monitoring

If a computer is an integral part of your job, you should be aware that there are many ways the employer can monitor your activities. Consider the following:

- *Screen or disk monitoring.* Some systems can show employers an exact image of what's on your screen or on a particular part of your hard drive. These systems are set up this way simply because employers own the computers and the network and are paying for your work in the office. System administrators within a company can be expected to have 100 percent access to everything on all employee computers that hasn't been encrypted by the employee.

- *Keystroke monitoring.* Some employers—especially those in intensive word-processing or data-entry environments— gauge the productivity of their workers by keystroke volume. They may use this information to evaluate overall performance or for comparison against expected averages. The downside of this activity is the added stress it often causes employees.

- *Idle-time monitoring.* Another monitoring technique involves the tracking of idle time—time spent by the employee away from the computer or involved in a nonwork activity at the computer.

- *Online monitoring.* Employers sometimes make use of Web-tracking software, which keeps a detailed log of Web sites visited, email exchanged, and newsgroups read. Some of these packages also have blocking capabilities that limit what sites can accessed from an employee's workstation.

Some employers notify staff members that monitoring is (or is not) taking place. This is a responsible practice, certainly, but it's neither required nor common. Since an employee can't be absolutely certain that monitoring in the workplace is *not* taking place, it's best to conduct oneself as if it were. It's certainly better to be safe in this regard than to discover during one's performance evaluation that such information has been collected. At that point it may be too late to remedy the problem, so asking about monitoring policies early in the work relationship is a good idea.

Employees are given some legal protection from computer and other forms of electronic monitoring, but only in specific circumstances. For U.S. government employees and people working under special union or personal contracts, for example, there are some limits on monitoring and constitutional protections against unreasonable search and seizure.

Email and Voicemail Monitoring

In most cases, email and voicemail in the workplace aren't private. Several court cases have determined that when an email system is used at a company, the employer owns it and may check the contents of it without telling employees. Messages transmitted internally, as well as those from outside the company, may therefore be subject to employer monitoring. This is also true for voicemail.

Email and voicemail systems retain messages (or traces of messages) even after they've been deleted. Messages that appear to have been erased often still exist, "backed up" and archived on magnetic tape by the system administrator. Even in the absence of backups, however, most deleted files can be recovered intact with a program such as Norton UnErase. Sensitive material should therefore be deleted with a file-wiping utility, which will overwrite the files numerous times with random data.

It's also important to remember that Internet email leaves "footprints" in its route to the recipient. After being sent, a message may still exist on the sender's machine, the recipient's machine, and a number of intermediate machines, from which it could be retrieved by government agents or other individuals with the access and the skills.

Even though an email system may have an option for marking messages "private," there's no real assurance that messages *are* being kept confidential (unless the company's written policy states otherwise). Even with a written commitment, if you have any doubts that your employer will stick to the policy, it's advisable to encrypt sensitive material. This ensures that your messages will be read only by your intended recipients.

While encryption may prevent snooping co-workers and outsiders from reading email, the employer may still have access to messages if he or she provides or controls the encryption. And that's often the case. Some employers *require* the use of encryption to protect the privacy of their employees' electronic mail (and therefore the company's secrets). And if they do, they often want to hold the key. After all, they have an interest in recovering work-related email if an employee leaves the company suddenly. Picture a legal defense sent back to square one because the attorney was hit by a bus, all his case files were encrypted, and the law firm didn't have a backup copy of the key. This doesn't mean that employers should have access to your own personal encryption keys, though they may have a justifiable policy against use of personal encryption products on company machines.

Workplace Privacy Protection

It's good insurance to become aware of your employer's workplace policies in regard to privacy. If your employer publishes those policies, they're considered legally binding. The place to look for these is usually in union contracts, administrative memos, or employee handbooks.

Currently there are very few laws regulating employee monitoring. If you're concerned about this issue, contact your federal legislators— especially the members of the House and Senate Labor committees (or your area's equivalent, if you're not in the United States). Several nonregulatory groups are actively involved in workplace monitoring issues as well, advocating stronger government regulation of employee monitoring. These groups include the following:

9 to 5 (The National Association of Working Women)
231 West Wisconsin Avenue, #900
Milwaukee, WI 53203
(414) 274-0925
(800) 522-0925 (job problems hotline)

American Civil Liberties Union
National Task Force on Civil Liberties in the Workplace
166 Wall Street
Princeton, NJ 08540
(609) 683–0313
http://www.aclu.org

The American Civil Liberties Union (ACLU) also has information available to the public on workplace privacy issues that aren't discussed in this book. Some of the issues of growing concern involve psychological testing, drug testing, and off-the-job surveillance of employees.

Additionally, the Electronic Frontier Foundation has drafted public-interest principles for filtration, labeling, rating, search-indexing, and agent processing of online information; these principles, available at *http://www.eff.org/policies,* speak in part to the use of monitoring and filtration software in the workplace.

Data and Network Security

Your company's network and data security are a subject of some complexity. The technical procedures necessary to provide safety (at various levels) have filled literally dozens of books. Many businesses today are primarily data businesses, and as such their very lifeblood is at stake in this area. If this is your field of professional concern, we recommend that you consult your technical bookstore, as well as the National Computer Security Association (*http://www.ncsa.com/*) and the Computer Security Institute (*http://www.gocsi.com/*) for professional publications and conferences.

Security Guidelines Questionnaire for the Workplace

How well protected is *your* company's sensitive information and equipment? Take the following questionnaire to find out:

- How well does your company limit physical access to sensitive information, whether in digital, paper, or other storage media?

- What procedures are in place to prevent former employees or outsiders from accessing company files?

- Is data security an area of assigned duty for specific staff members? How often do they participate in training and refresher courses or conferences on new developments?

- How often do you test your system (perhaps using a program such as Satan) to determine how difficult it is for it to be "hacked" or "cracked"?

- How do you ensure that your company's sensitive information is available only to authorized personnel? What types of segregation and disk security are in use?

- Do you employ an encryption policy? Is encryption used only for the most sensitive information, for personal information, or for anything that travels via the Internet?

- What are your company's procedures to protect against viruses?

- What are your company's procedures regarding passwords? Are employees required to change them often, and are they instructed in good password techniques?

- Do you utilize auditing procedures to avoid telephone fraud and theft of data and equipment? What are your penalty policies?

Cordless Phones, Cellular Phones, and Pagers

You might not think of wireless telephones as *new* media, but in many ways they are. Though providing you with conventional telephone service, these devices operate in ways that are substantially different from your wired desk phone, and thus present new privacy and regulatory issues. For example, it's fairly easy for others to listen in on calls made on cordless or cellular phones—and even pagers can be "intercepted." While wireless communications are very popular and have several advantages, privacy is not among them.

Wireless phone conversations are generally overheard by accident, and then only for brief periods. Still, some people do make a hobby out of eavesdropping on calls by using radio scanners (developed for use with CB and emergency bands); and of those people, another subset takes advantage of information thus gained. If you buy something over a cordless or cellular phone, giving your credit-card number and expiration date, and the call is monitored by an unsavory character, you may well end up the victim of credit-card fraud. Because of this danger, common sense tells us to avoid discussing financial or other sensitive personal information on wireless phones.

Cordless phones are actually low-powered radio stations. Radio waves transmit your conversation from the base unit to the handset and vice versa. Depending on the particular frequency your unit is using, you might be overheard on radio scanners, baby monitors, or other cordless phones in the vicinity. Although cordless phone signals usually extend only about a quarter of a mile at maximum, they're occasionally picked up as far as a couple of miles away.

Cellular phones, on the other hand, transmit and receive signals to and from a "cell site," which is a large antenna array serving an area up to twelve miles in radius. That cell site then connects your call to the wired telephone network. As you move during a conversation, a sensor tells the phone system that your signal is dropping in the cell you're leaving and growing stronger in the one you're moving into. A computerized switch then transfers your call between the cells. Usually this is done without any obvious audible effect. Cellular calls can't be heard on baby monitors or radios, but they can be heard by some scanners (despite a 1994 ruling by the Federal Communications Commission making manufacture of scanners in this frequency range illegal).

Most jurisdictions prohibit the "intentional" eavesdropping on cordless and cellular telephone conversations, or using a radio scanner "knowingly and with the intent to defraud" to eavesdrop on wire or electronic communications. (As a clear exception, if a law enforcement agency is investigating a specific crime, a judge can authorize the interception of a cellular call.) Penalties for the intentional interception of cordless and cellular telephone calls range from fines to imprisonment, depending on the circumstances.

Note that the concept of *intent* is integral to phone crime. To be a violation of the law, interception of cordless or cellular phone conversations must be done with malicious intent. This means that if your neighbor accidentally hears your conversation on a radio scanner, her actions aren't illegal. Furthermore, unless the eavesdropper says something about what she overheard, you have no way of knowing that your conversation was monitored.

How can you ensure wireless telephone privacy? Currently, there's no inexpensive way. If you need to discuss a private matter or simply don't want others to listen to your call, the only way to ensure privacy is to have both parties use a conventional wired telephone. However, you can do some things to minimize the chances that someone using a radio scanner will pick up your conversation. Cordless phones that offer ten or more channels and automatically switch to an unused channel when someone else comes on are far less likely to be picked up than the one- or two-channel models. Some of the newer models in the 900 MHz frequency range offer up to one hundred channels and are even less likely to be overheard.

Still better are digital cordless phones and digital cellular phone networks; these offer an even greater level of protection against eavesdropping than their analog siblings. In attempting to select the cordless or cellular phone that offers the most useful privacy features, compare published specifications and ask salespeople to assist by providing comparative information on the security features of the phones they sell.

Baby monitors, children's walkie-talkies, and some home intercom systems can be overheard in the same manner as cordless phones. If you're concerned about being overheard on one of these devices, be sure to turn it off when it's not in use (or purchase a wired unit instead).

Other Cellular Privacy Risks

According to the Cellular Telecommunications Industry Association, the cellular industry lost $482 million in 1994 to fraud. With the advent of digital cellular technology, this trend has begun to decline. One of the most common forms of cellular telephone fraud is the "cloning" of the electronic serial number (ESN) programmed into the cellular phone by the manufacturer. In an analog cellular telephone, the ESN and the mobile identification number (MIN) are generally used to identify a subscriber. One way the ESN is cloned is by capturing the ESN-MIN with a device called an ESN reader. The captured ESN-MIN is then reprogrammed into the computer chip of another cellular telephone. Digital cellular telephones provide more (but not total) security against cloning, because digital frequencies aren't as readily picked up by scanners.

The following are some steps you can take to prevent cellular telephone fraud:

1. If your phone has a lock feature, see that it's used when the phone isn't in service.

2. Review your cellular phone bills thoroughly and question any discrepancies.

3. Treat your phone's ESN as sensitive, confidential information and keep it in a safe place.

4. Ask your service provider what antifraud features are offered.

5. If your phone is stolen, report the theft immediately to both the cellular telephone carrier and the police.

Unfortunately, consumers usually learn about cellular telephone fraud only when they receive an alarming bill. Fortunately, standard industry practice is to not charge consumers for cloned calls. If you fall victim to cellular telephone fraud, contact your cellular telephone provider immediately. If you're having a problem with your service provider, file a complaint with the Federal Communications Commission, Enforcement Division, 2025 M Street Northwest, Washington, D.C. 20054, *http://www.fcc.gov.* A large repository of information on wireless telephony is available at the Web site of the Cellular Telecommunications Industry Association (*http://www.wow-com.com*).

> "**I**t's kind of the digital equivalent of a drive-by shooting."
>
> **A TEXAS A&M PROFESSOR** whose email account was abused by crackers who publicly posted racist remarks from the account, resulting in hatemail (including death threats) being sent to the professor; reported by the *Atlanta Journal Constitution,* October 19, 1994

Personal Communication Service Devices

Personal communication service (PCS) devices are pocket-sized wireless digital phones that transmit both voice and data. These cutting-edge devices bring both good and bad news regarding privacy. Because PCS networks transmit digitally, conversations are difficult (but not impossible) to intercept. But, like cellular phones, these devices can be used to pinpoint the caller's whereabouts. Will consumers want to carry a phone that knows where they are at all times? Will consumers want to be contacted anywhere at any time? As a society, we're still exploring the privacy implications of these new systems.

Fifteen Privacy-Protection Tools for Internet Users

What can I do to protect my privacy in cyberspace? you ask. When you're sitting alone at your computer, surfing the Internet, sending email messages, and participating in online forums, it's easy to be lulled into thinking that your activities are private. Be aware, though, that at any step along the way your online messages could be intercepted, and your activities monitored, in the vast uncivilized world of cyberspace.

1. Be a smart Internet service shopper. Research new services before registering with them. This can be done by participating in an appropriate newsgroup or through email discussion lists. Bad news travels fast in cyberspace, and you're likely to hear some very frank opinions from folks who've had experiences you can learn from. Of course, if you know the source of your references, you're able to gauge the credibility of the recommendations more accurately. One great way to make preliminary comparisons is by visiting the chart on major providers at *http://www.cdt.org/privacy/online_services/chart.html.*

2. If your provider isn't included on that chart (or perhaps even if it is), you should obtain the service's privacy policies in writing from the sysop and watch for messages relating to privacy that may appear on your screen during log-on. Read the latter very carefully, especially at your first log-on. Responsible service providers offer a clear policy to you in advance. Any provider that doesn't should be avoided.

3. Some service providers supply "startup" software that makes the first connection for you. You should be wary of these programs if they ask for credit-card, checking account, or other personal information before you can open an account. Often

they upload this data automatically as soon as the connection is made. They may be able to read other information as well, such as your system configuration, and upload that to the host computer without your knowledge. Some services have an alternative registration method you can utilize if you take the trouble to ask.

4. Your password is your first line of defense for security and privacy. Create passwords with nonsensical combinations of upper- and lowercase letters, numbers, and symbols—for example, gLi8&iX. Or, if you have trouble remembering that sort of combination, try something like L84dnr (which can be pronounced "late for dinner"). Change passwords often, don't write them down, don't let anyone watch you typing at log-on, and don't leave your computer unattended while you're logged on.

5. Remember that your online activities may be tracked by Web sites you visit, as well as your own service provider. Your provider has a record of the commands you've executed and the sites you've visited. Those sites may also be able to log your activity while you're there, especially in cases where you're asked to register or supply personal information. To avoid leaving digital footprints with your email, you can use anonymous remailers or an anonymizer (see *http://www.anonymizer.com*).

6. Be aware that erasing all traces of email is just about impossible. Simply clicking DELETE won't completely remove a message from the recipient's computer or from any of the machines it traveled through on its way. And even if you wipe it off your own computer, it may still be retrievable from a backup system.

7. Unless you use strong encryption, your communications online aren't private. Without such protection, you should be aware of the risks of sending personal data (such as addresses, passwords, credit-card numbers, or Social Security numbers) via email, and of revealing them in chat rooms, newsgroups, or in your online bio.

8. If an online bio is an optional feature with your service provider, remember that these bios can be searched and remotely read by anyone. If this exposure isn't comfortable to you for any reason, you should ask your sysop how to remove the file. You may also be able to purge your record from any online directory.

9. Keep in mind that newsgroup postings are usually archived for future reference. You can conduct a search for postings by a specific individual going back several years. This kind of record may be used to create a personal profile of you, which could subsequently be used by direct marketers or prospective employers.

10. Some providers allow you to select a list of favorite news-groups, or to prioritize those you like to visit. Remember that your system operator can monitor those lists. If you're concerned that your selections may be too sensitive or controversial for others to see, you're advised not to utilize this feature.

11. Be forewarned of the social risks of going online, such as flaming (using harsh, often colorful language), spamming (bulk-posting email), stalking, and harassment. Women are more likely to experience these problems than men, at least if they use an email address or online identity that identifies their gender. Taking an ID that's not gender-specific is usually an effective solution.

12. With the previous point in mind—the possibility of adopting an online identity—remember that the person you're corresponding with may not be who he or she claims to be.

13. Be especially helpful and involved if your children are online. Teach them the difference between appropriate and inappropriate conduct and suggest what to do if someone they're communicating with crosses the line. In addition, stress the importance of not revealing information about themselves or others in the family. Should it become an issue in your home, the National Center for Missing and Exploited Children is at *http://www.missingkids.org.*

14. If you publish information on a personal Web site, remember how public that information will be. If you'd rather not receive calls and junk mail from marketers, it's best not to publish descriptive information on your Web site.

15. Use privacy-protection tools. Several technologies, such as encryption and anonymous remailers, can help online users protect their privacy.

Reviewing Privacy Strategies

As we've seen, most of what we do on the Internet and in the workplace is equivalent to public communication; likewise, there's no guarantee that what transpires in the doctor's office or by phone will be private. We hope that this chapter has convinced you it's dangerous to think that you're anonymous on the Internet, or that you're acting privately just because you're alone at your computer. As we've noted, there are many people and organizations that have access to information about who you are and what you're doing online, at work, and by phone.

As a summary, let's restate some of the key points of this chapter:

- Guard personal data carefully, releasing it on the Internet only when necessary.

- When replying to email that you received via a "listserver," take care to see that the reply is addressed only to the individual who sent the original message. Otherwise, your reply (and any personal information attached to it) will go to the entire list.

- If a message that you had intended to be private becomes public, remember that another party to that message may have given consent for disclosure of its contents, permitting any sysop along its path to view it legally. You need to make sure of the circumstances before you take action against anyone.

- Educate yourself about what information is transmitted to remote computers by the software you use to browse remote sites.

- Always ask for the privacy policy of any online service you intend to use, and look for privacy statements at Web sites you visit.

- Participate in your own future: work in conjunction with private industry and law enforcement to formulate encryption options that balance the requirements of both liberty and security.

- Beware the abuses of anonymous remailers—they can be used to make threats or slander with impunity—but cherish the anonymity they offer.

- Don't assume that your medical records, or phone calls or faxes made by your health-care provider about your diagnosis and treatment, are private.

- Work with your legislators to ensure the confidentiality of health records.

- Remember the general rule regarding privacy in the workplace: *there is none.* Employers that don't have a stated policy to the contrary can be expected to monitor employee phone calls, email, and voicemail.

- The best way to ensure the privacy of your personal calls made at work is to use a pay phone or a separate phone designated by your employer for personal calls.

- Bear in mind that your organization's system administrator can be expected to have 100 percent access to everything unencrypted on all employee computers.

- Delete sensitive material from your office computer with a file-wiping utility, which overwrites deleted files numerous times with random data.

- Avoid discussing financial or other sensitive personal information on a cordless or cellular phone.

WEBLINKS TO THIS CHAPTER

There are a good many organizations working to protect what Internet privacy we now have and to make further privacy options available. Consult the following resources (some of which have been mentioned in this chapter) for further information:

American Health Information Management Association:
http://www.ahima.org

Anonymous Remailers
http://www.cs.berkeley.edu/~ralph/remailer-list.html

WEBLINKS TO THIS CHAPTER

(cont.)

U.S. Congress:
http://www.congress.org

the export of cryptography:
http://www.eff.org/pub/Privacy/ITAR_export/Bernstein_case/

EFF policies regarding workplace monitoring and filtering:
http://www.eff.org/policies

service provider policy comparison chart:
http://www.cdt.org/privacy/online_services/chart.html

everything wireless:
http://www.wow-com.com

EFF Privacy Archives:
http://www.eff.org/pub/Privacy/

Privacy Rights Clearinghouse:
http://www.privacyrights.org

Electronic Privacy Information Center (EPIC):
http://www.epic.org

Stanford University Privacy Info Links:
http://www-leland.stanford.edu/group/tdr-security/privacy.html

truste:
http://www.TRUSTe.org

Center for Democracy and Technology:
http://www.cdt.org

NOTES

1. Some of the information in this chapter was adapted from publications of the Privacy Rights Clearinghouse. For the full text of these and other documents, and for information on privacy rights in other areas, contact the Clearinghouse directly:

Privacy Rights Clearinghouse
5384 Linda Vista Road, Suite 306
San Diego, CA 92110
voice: (619) 298-3396
email: *prc@privacyrights.org*
http://www.privacyrights.org

See also *The Privacy Rights Handbook: How to Take Control of Your Personal Information,* by Beth Givens and the Privacy Rights Clearinghouse (Avon Books, 1997).

2. *Identity theft* refers to any attempt to fraudulently represent oneself as another individual, usually for the purpose of acquiring property or information in the name of the victim.

3. *Encryption,* as described in this chapter, is a means of encoding text or other data so that it can be read only by a recipient using the proper decryption key. Encryption is discussed in some detail later in the chapter.

4. For more information on encryption and privacy resources, visit the following Web sites:

http://www.pgp.com
http://www.junkbusters.com

5. The critical issue for public key cryptography is the strength of the underlying algorithm—the mathematical equation used to produce the encoding—which manifests in part as key length. As of mid-1997, the government's own Digital Encryption Standard (DES), a 56-bit cipher, was cracked by students and other Internet users who harnessed the spare time and processing power of numerous online computers. Even 56-bit encryption is subject to U.S. International Traffic in Arms Regulations export control. More recent 128-bit crypto programs are considered to be unbreakable with today's technology and are therefore also under U.S. government export restriction. Nonetheless, they're available in virtually every country on the planet.

6. You can download your copy of PGP and find out virtually anything you want to know about it by visiting either the main distribution Web site at Massachusetts Institute of Technology or the international home page:

http://Web.mit.edu/network/pgp.html
http://www.ifi.uio.no/pgp/

FOUR | COPYRIGHTS, LICENSES,
TRADEMARKS, AND PATENTS

Protecting Intellectual
Property Online

"Most Americans still can't figure out how to program their vcrs. They are not going to be able to get onto the World Wide Web and locate, on some obscure bulletin board, the latest copies of Microsoft's computer programs."

BRUCE LEHMAN, U.S. PATENT AND TRADEMARK OFFICE COMMISSIONER (on why he thinks current intellectual property law will last well into the next century)

Not a Moral Decision but a Business Strategy
by Esther Dyson

The Net poses interesting challenges both for owners/creators/sellers and for users of intellectual property (IP). Because it allows for essentially costless copying of content, it dramatically changes the economics of content. In this new world, competing with the old one, it will be easy to copy information, but hard to find it. It will be easy to program, but still hard to define the problems and questions that software programs must handle. Creativity will proliferate, but quality will be scarce and hard to recognize. Creators will have to fight to attract attention and to get paid. Logistics alone used to add value to IP; they do so no longer.

While content won't be entirely free, the economic dynamics will tend to operate as if it were. Content (including software) will serve as advertising for services such as support, aggregation, filtering, assembly, and integration of content modules or training—or it will be a by-product of paid-for relationships.

Because some of these terms, often used loosely, are crucial to an understanding of the complex issues surrounding intellectual property, let's define them here:

> *Content:* information, data, documents, images, and other digital media. This is the most inclusive term. Software usually falls into the content category unless the context indicates otherwise.
>
> *Intellectual property:* content, including software, defined by law as *protectable*. Its owner/creator has rights to define how it may be sold or used, and its integrity and authenticity are inviolable.
>
> *Intellectual value:* the value of intellectual property, whether or not it's legally protected. Basically, intellectual value is the benefit that content brings to users of that content; this is usually higher than the market value (which may be zero), since by definition no one will pay more than it's worth.
>
> *Market value:* what people are willing to pay for intellectual value.

For more from Esther Dyson, visit *http://www.edventure.com/release1/release1.html.*

In the age of information, virtually *everything* is intellectual property. And in the age of digital communication, *everything* is more easily reproducible and distributable, which brings into question our long-standing notions about legal protections for original works. When reduced to their smallest building blocks—those ones and zeros that comprise binary digital content—there's no difference between your résumé, someone's artwork, and a multi-million-dollar trade secret. Furthermore, unlike older "analog" copies (made via devices such as tape recorders and photocopiers), digital copies retain the quality and detail of the original item.

Digital communication brings with it a host of unprecedented questions and problems in the area of copyrights, patents, and trademarks, right along with all the wonderful new possibilities it opens up. Never before has it been possible to create and distribute your own work to a finely tuned (or even a mass) audience so easily or so cheaply. Before the Internet, distribution of original creative work lay almost exclusively in the hands of publishers and broadcasters, who controlled the channels that produced and distributed the work. Before movable type and the printing press, the channels were controlled by the clergy or the elder storytellers of the community. Now it's wide open, with one-to-many and many-to-many communication readily available in our shrinking global community.

Online services such as America Online and CompuServe have contractual provisions stipulating that the copyright for all original creations uploaded onto their public areas is partially owned by the service. (The term "creations" excludes your email and other private or one-to-one communications.) These services also permit writers to adopt an online identity that prevents others from knowing their true identity. At the other extreme is WELL (Whole Earth 'Lectronic Link), one of the oldest online conferencing services. Its policy, known as YOYOW (You Own Your Own Words), takes no responsibility for the postings of members and permits no anonymity. Each member's true identity is available in the service's public record. As you might imagine, these policies foster very different community behaviors, but they do have something important in common: informed consent. People considering membership with any of these services are given the rules in advance and allowed the opportunity to decide if they're comfortable with them. This is an excellent fundamental principle for community-building online.

The ease with which digital information can be copied and distributed is great news for independent writers, programmers, musicians, and photographers who want to get their works out into the world. There's bad news too, however: plagiarism and unauthorized redistribution of work can spell disaster to those who depend on being compensated directly for their creations. In the past, these issues have been the subject of traditional copyright law—a legal means of deterring and punishing those who would "steal" intellectual property for their own purposes.

Copyright Protection

The full history and application of copyright law is beyond the scope of this book, but it's important to know the basics about how it's applied so that you can protect your own work and avoid being hauled into court for infringing someone else's rights. (Breaking the copyright law today can carry penalties of fifty thousand dollars for each infringed work, along with attorney's fees, court costs, criminal fines, and imprisonment. And neither ignorance of the statutes nor innocent intent is an acceptable defense.) The brief history that follows, focused narrowly in the interest of brevity, emphasizes the copyrighting of software.

The Evolution of Copyright Law

The first copyright law appeared in about 1570; it was an act of the British Parliament called the Statute of Anne. At that time there were books and illustrations only—no digital multimedia or software programs, of course. It was 1790 before the first U.S. statute was on the books, offering similar protection. Using this early law, and its many revisions, as the basis for their decision, the first courts to evaluate software for copyright questioned whether programs or digital information could be copyrighted at all. The judges—unable to read the programs—wondered if material that was only machine-readable deserved the same protections as other human expression.

In 1980, the United States enacted a federal law known as the Software Act, which modified existing copyright protection by including software programs as protected under the Copyright Act. U.S. copyright law must be in accordance with Article I, Section 8, of the Constitution. The first such law was passed in 1790, with major revisions in 1831, 1870, 1909, and 1976. An initial term of twenty-eight years can be renewed to extend fifty years after the death of the work's creator. The Universal Copyright Convention was signed in Geneva, Switzerland, in 1952. Thirty-six nations agreed to give international protection to scientific works, artistic works, and literature. The U.S. signed on in 1955. There are a few exceptions to that protection, but they're insignificant to this discussion. The next piece of the law's evolution came in the case of *Apple* v. *Franklin*, in which it was determined that copyright protection exists even if the program in question is stored only in ROM (computer memory) rather than on paper.

Copyright is understood to be the right to duplicate and/or show a work, and the right to prohibit others from doing likewise. It's an exclusive right with five components:

1. The exclusive right to make copies.

2. The exclusive right to distribute copies to the public.

3. The exclusive right to prepare derivative works.

4. The exclusive right to perform the work in public.

5. The exclusive right to display the work in public.

When no one can legally claim the above rights, a work may be said to be in "public domain." This description wouldn't apply to something such as "shareware," in which a program is copyrighted but distributed at no cost (with a request for donations).

When you buy a software program or access to online information, you're buying a single copy of that information for your use or enjoyment (unless you have a license to the contrary from the copyright holder). You haven't bought the right to *reproduce* it. Still, the first thing that happens when you download a Web page or insert a disk into your floppy drive is that your computer makes a copy of it (with certain exceptions). Making a copy of a program in RAM is allowed for by the Software Act, however, if the copy "is created as an essential step in the utilization of the computer program in conjunction with a machine and . . . is used in no other manner. . . ." Not so clearly addressed by the law are questions as to whether that software can be run on a network of several machines or whether such a network should instead be considered a "public performance" (as in the fourth right listed above).

In consideration of the new and unique properties of software programs, copyright law was further revised to allow one "archive" copy of the program (in addition to the RAM copy that the computer makes automatically). This backup copy is for archival purposes only; it's not to be given to an associate, enabling two users to get it for the price of one. However, should you decide that you wish to sell or lend a software program to someone, you may do so, as long as you don't keep the backup copy yourself. (Although, as we noted, the copyright holder has the exclusive right to distribute or sell

> **"Digital technology is the universal solvent of intellectual property rights."**
>
> TOM PARMENTER,
> *DESPERADO*, Issue 12

copies of the software, that right applies only to the first sale of a particular copy. The same is true for books, records, and the like.)

Modification of Copyrighted Digital Media

Let's say that you're a brilliant artist with an image-processing program that allows you to do incredible things with a photographic image. And let's say that you found a beautiful—but copyrighted—image of a sunset in an online library. And let's say further that you made a wonderful collage out of that image, incorporating several other copyrighted images as well. What's the legal status of your actions?

Well, technically you've infringed the copyright of each picture you "borrowed" by making a derivative work without permission. Of course, unless you distribute your own creation by uploading it somewhere, or publishing it, you're not likely to experience any litigation. The same holds true for music and text creations adapted in some way from another source.

With regard to application software programs, some modification is allowed for your own use: a clause in the Software Act states that an adaptation made by the user (presumably to improve a program's performance) is allowed without permission of the copyright owner if the adaptation "is created as an essential step in the utilization of the computer program in conjunction with a machine"—namely, the user's computer.

Incidentally, to help identify copyright owners and facilitate the permissions process in the digital world, many programs, such as Photoshop and most music-authoring programs, now feature a "digital watermark." This serves as a signature, affixing information about the copyright holder (somewhat permanently) to the original file. If you download or receive a work and are unsure of its copyright status, you'd be well advised to check for a watermark or other copyright notice before redistributing or modifying it.

Protecting Your Work with Copyright

If you're wondering how to go about getting copyright protection, you may be surprised to learn that if you've authored an original work, you *already* hold the copyright! If you made it, you own it—that is, until there's a dispute over that ownership and you're asked to show proof. The best way to ensure proof of ownership is to register your work with the U.S. Copyright Office. Not a requisite, but certainly advisable. The other thing you must do is include a copyright notice on every copy that you distribute by any means. If you don't, a recipient can legally assume that the material is in the public domain. The next thing you know, a court may be determining that you've *lost* your copyright.

The copyright notice has three parts. The first can be either a *c* with a circle around it ©, the word *Copyright,* or the abbreviation *Copr.* The *c* with a circle around it is preferable, because that symbol is recognized around the world; the other variations aren't. That's a very important detail. Countries around the world have agreed to recognize and uphold each other's copyrights, but this worldwide protection requires the use of the ©. On disk labels and program packaging, use ©; in code and on the screen, use *Copyright* or *Copr.* if you can't make a circle. (Computers don't draw small circles well, so programmers and online authors have resorted to using a *c* in parentheses: (c). Unfortunately, that has no legal meaning.)

The second part of the notice is the "year of first publication of the work." *Publication,* in the context of software, doesn't mean distribution by XYZ Publishing Co.; it means distribution of copies of the program to the public "by sale or other transfer of owner-ship, or by rental, lease, or lending." So when you start handing out or selling copies of your precious work, you're publishing. In fact, publication takes place when you merely *offer* to distribute copies to a group for further distribution. Your copyright notice must include the year that you first did any of these things.

The third part of the notice is the name of the owner of the copyright. If that's you, your last name will do. If your company owns the program, the company name is appropriate.

Here's an example of a legal copyright notice:

Copyright © 1998 Verbum, Inc.

Where do you put the notice? Where people are likely to see it. On the Web, it's a good idea to put it on every page. If you're dis-tributing a human-readable code listing, put the notice on the first page in the first few lines of code and hard-code it so that it appears on the title screen, or at sign-off, or continuously. If you're distributing machine-readable versions only, hard-code the notice. As an extra precaution, you should also place the notice on the gummed disk label or attach it permanently to the storage medi-um in some other fashion.

Registering your copyright for a computer program, a photograph, or a written document may not seem important to you unless and until someone else takes your work and makes money from it. If that ever happens, however, you'll be glad you took the time to register with the U.S. Copyright Office. If you can prove that you registered your work before the infringement took place, you may be entitled to large statutory damages, and the court could order the offender to pay your attorney's fees. Registration costs only ten dollars and can easily be done by a private citizen. For details on registration, visit *http://lcweb.loc.gov/copyright/;* write to the Register of Copyrights, Copyright Office, Library of Congress, Washington, D.C. 20559-6000; or phone (202) 707-9100.

Transferring Your Copyright

There are two ways that ownership of a copyright can legally shift from you, as author, to another person or organization. The first way is automatic: absent a provision to the contrary, you give up the copyright if you create a product as a "work for hire." The second way is voluntary: you can sell or assign the copyright to some person or organization.

Most (if not all) of what you create while at work is the property of the employer, especially if you're creating a product that's central to the business of that company. This transfer of copyright is almost automatic; no special written agreement is required for it to take place. On the other hand, if you're able to convince your employer to let you retain ownership of copyright, you must get that agreement in writing.

You may have a legitimate claim to copyright of work done in the workplace if it was created "outside of the scope of your job" and done without the use of the employer's facilities. Employment contracts sometimes attempt to get around this exception by stipulating that the employer is the owner of original products created off the job as well as on. In many states, though, such contracts aren't considered valid.

If you're an independent contractor, things are quite different. Your product isn't considered a "work for hire" in that case unless there's a written agreement between the parties that says so and that names the product as a specifically commissioned work. To meet the criteria for "commissioning," your work must fall into one of the following categories:

- A contribution to a collective work

- An audiovisual work (such as a computer game)

- A translation

- An instructional text

- A test or an answer to a test

- An atlas

Let's look at an example. If you're a game programmer and you live in California (or a number of states with similar laws), and if you sign an agreement that commissions you to create a new game and describes that game as a "work for hire," then the company owns the copyright. However (and it's a big however), the law also defines this type of arrangement as *employment,* meaning that you're entitled to certain benefits, such as worker's compensation and unemployment insurance. You'll need to consult your own state's employment laws for more details.

License and Law in Conflict

When you purchase software, either on a disk or downloaded from the Internet, you're generally given a license to use that software. In packaged software, the license is usually on a seal you must break to access the disks ("shrinkwrap license"); at online sites, you usually

have to click a button that indicates your acceptance of the manufac-
turer's terms ("clickwrap license"). The reason for this license is to
further limit your use of that software. Some licenses prohibit the
making of archive copies, for example, although the copyright law
specifically allows it. In cases such as this, where the license and the
law conflict, the terms of the license that you actively or passively
agree to may be considered binding—but not necessarily. This is one
of those areas where there's little agreement, especially between jurisdictions. Clickwrap licenses are subject to greater controversy than
shrinkwrap licenses, in part because they're newer; but they'll probably soon be the subject of specific legislation designed to reduce
ambiguity. If you must be certain about the licensing of particular
software, we suggest that you consult a library or attorney in your
locality.

The Fair-Use Doctrine

The most significant limitation on protection by copyright comes
from the "fair-use doctrine," a legal provision for purposes such as
criticism, comment, news reporting, teaching (as in copies for class-
room use), scholarship, and research. The U.S. law "permits and
requires courts to avoid rigid application of the copyright statute
when, on occasion, it would stifle the very creativity which that law is
designed to foster."

This doctrine is what allows news and educational media to incorporate portions of a copyrighted work in reportage, and what allows
satirists to publicly perform (or make a derivative parody of) otherwise copyrighted work in the process of critically commenting on the
original piece.

The U.S. Congress has enumerated four nonexclusive criteria that
must be considered in determining whether a potential infringement
falls under the doctrine of fair use:

1. The purpose and character of the use, including whether such use is of a commercial nature or is for nonprofit educational purposes

2. The nature of the copyrighted work

3. The amount and substantiality of the portion used in relation to the copyrighted work as a whole

4. The effect of the use upon the potential market for or value of the copyrighted work

The fair-use doctrine calls for a case-by-case analysis, with all of the above factors weighed together in light of the purposes of copyright.

Trademark and Patent Protection

Trademark registration is a way of protecting a unique identity for a company, an organization, or a product/service. It applies most obviously to names but sometimes also covers both the graphic representation of a name and an image that symbolizes or encapsulates a product or corporation or publication. As in any publishing medium, those putting their trademarks online need to be aware of the ease with which a treasured name or image can be pirated, the speed with which an identity (built up over years) can be diluted or destroyed. If your trademark is registered, it should always carry the registration mark when it appears online, its ownership thereby announced and defended as it would be in print or broadcast media.

The new world of networked communication makes protection of a trademark (like protection of a copyright) much more difficult, even as it makes awareness of it easier. A great place to become knowledgeable about trademark law and cyberspace is *http://www. law.cornell.edu/topics/trademark.html.*

One of the more noteworthy controversies on the Internet in recent years has been the conflict over domain names. In an Internet address, the second-level domain (the "eff" in *www.eff.org*) is a valuable link to a company or product trademark. Before the commercial explosion of the World Wide Web, we rarely heard of a conflict over these domains; but in the past several years, with the flood of businesses jumping on the Net, there have been numerous requests for the same domain name (and even a rash of "pirated" domains, registered by opportunists who hoped to sell them for high fees). The list of companies that have had their names pirated before they could register them includes McDonald's, Coke, Hertz, Nasdaq, Viacom, MTV, Avon, Levi Strauss, B. Dalton, and Reader's Digest.

NSI, a U.S. company once officially designated to assign domain names,[1] developed a policy for resolving disputes that says, in effect, that the owner of a trademark registered in the United States or in a foreign county (state registration isn't sufficient) can challenge the use of an identical second-level domain by submitting the registration certificate to NSI, along with proof that the trademark owner has sent the domain holder written notice of the trademark owner's claim that the use and registration of the domain name violates the trademark owner's legal rights. If the first use of the domain postdates the first use of the trademark or the effective date of the trademark registration (whichever is earlier), then NSI gives the domain holder thirty days to prove its ownership of trademark registration for the same mark in the United States or any foreign country.

If the domain holder is able to prove either (1) that its use of the domain predates both the first use of the challenging party's registration and the effective date of that registration or (2) that the domain holder has its own trademark registration, then the domain holder is able to keep the domain (subject to the policies of the various

Internet authority groups). If the domain holder *can't* demonstrate the required prior domain use or produce a trademark registration certificate, then the domain holder must give up the domain within a ninety-day transition period.[2] The domain in question is then "frozen," not available to anyone, pending the outcome of the dispute between the parties.

It's important to note that having a second-level domain registered with NSI in the United States doesn't prevent the same second-level domain being used with a different top-level domain in another country, such as *.uk* in the United Kingdom, *.ca* in Canada, or *.au* in Australia, to name a few.

The complex and problem-ridden domain-name system on the Net is slated for a complete overhaul at the time of this writing. Various Internet working committees have drafted proposals aiming to standardize a broader naming system and a more decentralized network of registration organizations. It may be some time until this process is completed, however, because it's turned into a power struggle.

The domain-name tug-of-war began after the release of a proposal by a temporary working group called the Internet International Ad Hoc Committee (IAHC). It was their intent to plan a system to succeed the NSI contract after March 1998. The IAHC was comprised of representatives from the following groups whose work impacts the use of the Net: Internet Society (ISOC), Internet Assigned Numbers Authority (IANA), Internet Architecture Board (IAB), Federal Networking Council (FNC), International Telecommunication Union (ITU), International Trademark Association (INTA), and World Intellectual Property Organization (WIPO).

Apparently, this international planning group didn't represent certain nations well enough, as there were groups in Europe and Japan that protested being excluded. Other businesses with a vested interest in how top-level domains are determined registered their discontent and formed an alternate ad hoc committee with the intent of submitting their own proposal and fighting what they felt was an unfair power grab by the original committee. And even though this is a global infrastructure, the U.S. Congress and White House have held hearings on the matter in anticipation of legislation to "manage" the Internet. Whether the U.S. can claim such authority is an entire debate by itself.

Since the operation of everything on the Net depends on a stable domain-name and IP address system, it is likely that the leaders of these organizations will find common ground on which to build a consensus that enables the Net to continue without disruption. The salient point here is the way this scenario demonstrates how this giant network has developed, without centralized management, and through consensus, to achieve functionality.

For now, the questions remain: how will domains be registered, and by whom? There are also the greater questions of who will govern the Internet? And under what authority?

Feds Nab Domain Thief

In a colorful demonstration of protest, one which underscores just how wild this frontier is, a man named Eugene Kashpureff "hijacked" Net users accessing the InterNIC server. This act, which affected thousands of users and businesses, was supposedly intended as a protest against Network Solutions and the current system of registering domains. With a clever job of hacking and spoofing, the computer which maintains the records for top-level domains (such as .com, .org, .edu) was taken off the Net and replaced with another, dubbed by its creator as AlterNIC.

For about 120 hours in July of 1997, Kashpureff's AlterNIC operated in place of InterNIC. Here is what happened:

The Domain Name System is the method for converting host

names—such as *www.hacked.com*—into their associated Internet Protocol (IP) numerical addresses. As is common on the Net, this function is distributed across thousands of computers, working together to provide information about local domains.

When you browse the Web or look for email, your computer first sends a query to a name server, to which the reply will be that host's IP address. But when the IP address is returned, additional information may also be sent. Most DNS clients, such as browsers and FTP programs, will simply accept the additional data as valid and save it, without verifying.

The additional data may concern any top-level domain, or, as in this case, existing domains can be redirected to anywhere else on the Net. We don't have specifics as to what sites were replaced beyond InterNIC, but clearly, via this means, a hacker can take a domain offline, switch addresses between any two sites, and thereby totally disrupting the Net.

Kashpureff was quoted in the press as feeling he had not broken any laws. Indeed, he made no secret of who was responsible, or how it was done. Apparently, the U.S. Federal Bureau of Investigation disagreed, and in November of 1997 arrested him for wire fraud.

Experts are concerned that details of this attack are available on the Net, and that nearly every machine connected to it is vulnerable.

Predictably, intellectual property disagreements are at the heart of the controversy. There's considerable controversy over patents and the new media as well. Some intellectual property may indeed be patentable; however, this form of protection, intended for inventions and their derivative applications, doesn't work well in the fast-paced world of networked communication. The slow-moving patent process gives the owner exclusive rights to make, use, or sell an item for seventeen years. Although it's rarely granted to software applications, some programmers attempt to secure this means of protection.

Many programmers (and attorneys, for that matter) believe that the United States and other countries that recognize software patents as valid are in error. They contend that the rapid pace with which software is developed is essentially incompatible with the patent system. While such statements may be sweeping, the many cases we've seen of "submarine patents"—what we might call "hidden" patents encompassing some broad area of technology (for example, multimedia technology)—indicate that there's merit to at least some of these arguments. The typical submarine patent is granted with little fanfare, years before it's useful. Then, when the technology in question has been reinvented many times over and applied globally, the original patent holder suddenly surfaces (like a submarine—hence the label) to demand massive amounts of money in licensing revenues.[3]

If you'd like more information on trademarks and patents, you'll find a great deal at *http://www.uspto.gov.*

Original Database Protection

A database is yet another category of intellectual property. A digital database is a collection of information stored on a computer so that it can be selectively searched and the desired information retrieved by a few keystrokes. Manual databases, such as the telephone book and reference books, have been around since publishing began. Now, with the new digital media having made the search and retrieval process so much easier, digital databases by the score have become essential tools for businesses and consumers.

Since both the accumulation and the organization of information in databases require a significant amount of work, and since that work may involve original creative thought and execution, some databases are protected under the Copyright Act. The Copyright Office follows case law in this matter, sometimes allowing databases to be considered literary works (compilations), although they're not specifically included in the statutes. As literary works, databases have four components that are potentially protected:

1. Selection of the content

2. Internal coordination of the content

3. Arrangement of all elements of the database

4. The content itself

The copyright may apply to any of these parts of a literary work without including the others. Indeed, in the case of databases, it usually does, since the information contained in a database is so often public knowledge—just facts, not "ownable" by the compiler. For example, if you were to call up all the book publishers in every phone book you could get your hands on to determine which of them published books on computers, the ones who replied positively could be put into a database that would possibly be unique. The names and addresses of the publishers wouldn't be protectable; the way they were organized, if simply alphabetical, wouldn't be protectable; but the unique information about their specialization *might* be protectable. If you went to all the trouble of accumulating and sorting this information, you wouldn't want a competitor to benefit from your work; you'd want him to have to invest similar resources to acquire the information himself. That's a major reason that courts allow protection of this kind of work.

In a well-publicized case (*Rural Telephone* v. *Feist Publications*), a phone company sued for infringement against another publisher of a phone directory, proving that Feist had simply copied Rural's white-page listings, seeding the listings with fictitious entries to conceal their offense. Rural argued that listings of phone numbers and addresses, though obviously factual information, were protected under the copyright registration of the phone book. They argued that Feist should be required to go to the same effort rather than simply benefiting from Rural's previous work. The trial court agreed, entering a judgment for Rural; but Feist, appealing all the way to the U.S. Supreme Court, got a reversal. The justices found that the white pages weren't protected—they lacked the originality that must be present for copyright, it was determined—although the rest of the book was protected. In other words, copyright rewards originality, not just "sweat of the brow" effort.

If you're concerned about protecting an original database, there are alternatives to copyright, such as contractual protection. For more in-depth information on this subject, we suggest that you visit the Information Law Web site at *http://tsw.ingress.com/tsw/rcl/infolaw.html*.[4]

Jurisdictional Confusion

Now that you've educated yourself and registered all your copyrights, patents, and trademarks, you're in for a splash of cold water. Even before digital communication, the copyright system was far from wonderful. With the new technology, it's troubled indeed. While proponents still see it as necessary and even helpful, there are some very bright minds who feel that it's only a matter of time until the system dissolves in digital space. They argue that the concept of copyright addresses only the issue of regulating physical copies—an issue bearing only indirect relationship to life online. They predict that concepts going beyond limiting the availability of works will be crucial in the new age. (See, for example, the comments by J. P. Barlow, below.)

But you're here *today*, doing business on the Net, governed by current laws. Say you've just discovered (to your surprise) an original copyrighted photograph of yours on a Web site located somewhere in Finland. What do you do? The photo was taken from your own Web site in the United States, made available on a server in Scandinavia, and perpetuated in virtually every country on the planet via an ethereal place called cyberspace. To whom do you complain? Who has jurisdiction for infringement in cases like this?

Protecting your copyright is usually a matter of contacting the "infringer," informing them of your rights over the material in question, and requesting that they comply with international law by either ceasing use of the material, paying an appropriate fee, or, in some cases, both. If the reply and subsequent actions do not satisfy your request, your next recourse is in the courts. Since courts are costly, in some cases even to those winning judgments, it's best to consider carefully whether a lawsuit will ultimately be worthwhile. On the other hand, if continuing to hold the copyright is important to you, it may be necessary to get that judgment in any event, otherwise a subsequent infringer might point to the first case as demonstrating your work has been in the public domain.

Copyright infringement cases are very different from many other potential Net crimes in that there are some common international standards. That commonality is missing in some arenas. For example, posting a photo on the Net of a woman in a bathing suit, perfectly legal in most countries, would be a crime in Saudi Arabia.

So even if you can't decide at first who has jurisdiction in your case of the purloined photograph, at least you know that the copyright law in Finland is comparable to that of the United States. Thanks to a treaty called the Berne Convention for the Protection of Literary and Artistic Works (1886), there's a global standard for copyright protection (though there are, of course, some exceptions). Countries that are signatories to the treaty offer copyright protection and reciprocation in cases of infringement from other signed nations. For more information on the Berne Convention, visit *http://eff.org/pub/ Intellectual_property/us_berne_convention.paper.*

More recently, we've seen the founding of the World Intellectual Property Organization (WIPO), a United Nations intergovernmental group headquartered in Geneva, Switzerland. WIPO was created to promote and protect intellectual property throughout the world through cooperation among its member states, and to deal with various multilateral treaties addressing the legal and administrative aspects of intellectual property. The organization consists of over 150 nations, including all members of the European Union, the countries of Eastern Europe, the United States, and China. Basing its work on existing international treaties—primarily the Berne Convention and the Rome Convention for the Protection of Performers, Producers of Phonograms, and Broadcasting Organizations—a WIPO conference in Geneva in December 1996 adopted two agreements (the WIPO Copyright Treaty and the WIPO Performances and Phonograms Treaty).

To become law, these agreements must be ratified by member states, which then must appropriately modify their national legislation. While it's not mandatory that they do this, it's expected that major member states (including the United States) will. For more information, visit *http://www.wipo.org.*

False Security

With all the discussion of laws, treaties, international organizations, and reciprocity in these pages, we may have given you the wrong impression—the impression that intellectual property can be protected from theft. If you follow any of the traditional paths to protecting intellectual property, you'll likely end up with a false sense of security, at least as far as the digital media go. When all is said and done, the cost and effort required to defend your property rights in cyberspace would probably be better spent in the pursuit of improving your product, distributing it as widely as possible, and solidifying relationships with your patrons and customers.

In the midst of the confusion that now surrounds intellectual property and the Net, one thing is pretty well assured: we need to rethink our definitions of property, value, and the jurisdictions in which they dwell. The following excerpt from an article by EFF co-founder John Perry Barlow puts these issues in clear perspective and gives us the basis for a new way of looking at intellectual property.

From "Selling Wine Without Bottles: Economy of Mind on the Global Net"
by John Perry Barlow

. . . The increasing difficulty of enforcing existing copyright and patent laws is already placing in peril the ultimate source of intellectual property, the free exchange of ideas.

That is, when the primary articles of commerce in a society look so much like speech as to be indistinguishable from it, and when the traditional methods of protecting their ownership have become ineffectual, attempting to fix the problem with broader and more vigorous enforcement will inevitably threaten freedom of speech.

The greatest constraint on your future liberties may come not from government but from corporate legal departments laboring to protect by force what can no longer be protected by practical efficiency or general social consent. . . .

In Cyberspace, there are not only no national or local boundaries to contain the scene of a crime and determine the method of its prosecution, there are no clear cultural agreements on what a crime might be. Unresolved and basic differences between European and Asian cultural assumptions about intellectual property can only be exacerbated in a region where many transactions are taking place in both hemispheres and yet, somehow, in neither. . . .

What is to be done? While there is a certain grim fun to be had in it, dancing on the grave of copyright and patent will solve little, especially when so few are willing to admit that the occupant of this grave is even deceased and are trying to uphold by force what can no longer be upheld by popular consent.

The legalists, desperate over their slipping grip, are vigorously trying to extend it. Indeed, the United States and other proponents of GATT are making adherence to our moribund systems of intellectual property protection a condition of membership in the marketplace of nations. For example, China will be denied Most Favored Nation trading status unless they agree to uphold a set of culturally alien principles which are no longer even sensibly applicable in their country of origin. . . .

Familiarity Has More Value Than Scarcity

With physical goods, there is a direct correlation between scarcity and value. Gold is more valuable than wheat, even though you can't eat it. While this is not always the case, the situation with information is usually precisely the reverse. Most soft goods increase in value as they become more common. Familiarity is an important asset in the world of information. It may often be the case that the best thing you can do to raise the demand for your product is to give it away.

While this has not always worked with shareware, it could be argued that there is a connection between the extent to which commercial software is pirated and the amount which gets sold. Broadly pirated software, such as Lotus 1-2-3 or WordPerfect,

becomes a standard and benefits from the Law of Increasing
Returns based on familiarity. . . .

One of the aspects of the electronic frontier which I have
always found most appealing—and the reason Mitch Kapor and I
used that phrase in naming our foundation—is the degree to
which it resembles the nineteenth-century American West in its
natural preference for social devices which emerge from its conditions rather than those which are imposed from the outside.

Until the West was fully settled and "civilized" in this century,
order was established according to an unwritten Code of the
West, which had the fluidity of etiquette rather than the rigidity
of law. Ethics were more important than rules. Understandings
were preferred over laws, which were, in any event, largely unen-
forceable.

I believe that law, as we understand it, was developed to protect
the interests which arose in the two economic "waves" which
Alvin Toffler accurately identified in [his book] *The Third Wave*.
The First Wave was agriculturally based and required law to order
ownership of the principal source of production, land. In the
Second Wave, manufacturing became the economic mainspring,
and the structure of modern law grew around the centralized institutions which needed protection for their reserves of capital, man-
power, and hardware.

Both of these economic systems required stability. Their laws
were designed to resist change and to assure some equability of
distribution within a fairly static social framework. The possibility
spaces had to be constrained to preserve the predictability necessary to either land stewardship or capital formation.

In the Third Wave we have now entered, information to a large
extent replaces land, capital, and hardware, and . . . information is
most at home in a much more fluid and adaptable environment.

The Third Wave is likely to bring a fundamental shift in the purposes and methods of law which will affect far more than simply those statutes which govern intellectual property.

The "terrain" itself—the architecture of the Net—may come to serve many of the purposes which could only be maintained in the past by legal imposition. For example, it may be unnecessary to constitutionally assure freedom of expression in an environment which, in the words of my fellow EFF co-founder, John Gilmore, "treats censorship as a malfunction" and re-routes proscribed ideas around it.

Similar natural balancing mechanisms may arise to smooth over the social discontinuities which previously required legal intercession to set right. On the Net, these differences are more likely to be spanned by a continuous spectrum which connects as much as it separates.

And, despite their fierce grip on the old legal structure, companies which trade in information are likely to find that in their increasing inability to deal sensibly with technological issues, the courts will not produce results which are predictable enough to be supportive of long-term enterprise. Every litigation becomes like a game of Russian roulette, depending on the depth of the presiding judge's clue-impairment.

Uncodified or adaptive "law," while as "fast, loose, and out of control" as other emergent forms, is probably more likely to yield something like justice at this point. In fact, one can already see in development new practices to suit the conditions of virtual commerce. The life forms of information are evolving methods to protect their continued reproduction.

For example, while all the tiny print on a commercial diskette envelope punctiliously requires much of those who would open it, there are, as I say, few who read those provisos, let alone follow them to the letter. And yet, the software business remains a very healthy sector of the American economy.

Why is this? Because people seem to eventually buy the software they really use. Once a program becomes central to your work, you want the latest version of it, the best support, the actual manuals, all privileges which are attached to ownership. Such practical considerations will, in the absence of working law, become more and more important in getting paid for what might easily be obtained for nothing.

I do think that some software is being purchased in the service of ethics or the abstract awareness that the failure to buy it will result in its not being produced any longer, but I'm going to leave those motivators aside. While I believe that the failure of law will almost certainly result in a compensating re-emergence of ethics as the ordering template of society, this is a belief I don't have room to support here.

Instead, I think that . . . compensation for soft products will be driven primarily by practical considerations, all of them consistent with the true properties of digital information, where the value lies in it, and how it can be both manipulated and protected by technology.

While the conundrum remains a conundrum, I can begin to see the directions from which solutions may emerge, based in part on broadening those practical solutions which are already in practice. . . .

The full text of the above article is available at *http://eff.org/pub/Intellectual_property/idea_economy.article.*

WEBLINKS TO THIS CHAPTER

copyright:
http://lcweb.loc.gov/copyright

TRUSTe:
http://www.truste.org

legal:
http://tsw.ingress.com/tsw/rcl/infolaw.html

Esther Dyson:
http://www.edventure.com/release1/release1.html

Barlow article:
http://eff.org/pub/Intellectual_property/idea_economy.article

trademarks:
http://www.law.cornell.edu/topics/trademark.html

patent and trademark office:
http://www.uspto.gov

Berne Convention:
http://eff.org/pub/Intellectual_property/us_berne_convention.paper

World Intellectual Property Organization:
http://www.wipo.org

NOTES

1. Although no organization is responsible for managing the Net, certain working groups have developed to agree on standards and to handle business that would otherwise be chaotic (some say it is anyway). In 1993, the National Science Foundation, one of the Internet's founding organizations, announced it was abandoning its role as domain-naming authority. InterNIC, the Internet Network Information Center, was created as a collaborative project between General Atomics and AT&T and Network Solutions, Inc. Each had a five-year agreement with the NSF. General Atomics had responsibility for the

Information Services Project, AT&T was responsible for the InterNIC Directory and Database Services Project, and NSI was to handle domain-name registration. At the time of this printing, those agreements are about to expire, and no replacement system has yet been agreed upon. A number of different factions in the Internet community have attempted to stake claim to the domain-naming process, yet it is not even clear who has the authority to settle a dispute in this territory.

2. Many have criticized the NSI policy as essentially usurping the authority of the courts to decide whose claims are valid. Those critics claim that because NSI is a government contractor, its actions in this regard should be considered the unconstitutional taking of property without compensation.

3. Another patent-related controversy is the even more rare issuance of algorithm patents. Very few countries recognize patents on algorithms, but one that does is the United States—the country that also, incidentally, houses much of the most advanced cryptography research. The problem lies in granting a patent for a mathematical algorithm—a property of nature—rather than for a particular invention or program that utilizes that algorithm. Critics of algorithm patenting perhaps rightly point out that this is akin to granting a competitor a monopolistic right to "2 + 2 = 4" or to gravity. In any case, algorithm patenting has led to a concentration of market power in a very few hands in the U.S. cryptography industry.

4. In 1997, the United Nation's World Intellectual Property Organization (WIPO) examined a draft database-protection treaty but rejected it after loud public, academic, and commercial outcry. Critics claimed that such a treaty, like algorithm patents, would give corporations complete ownership over particular facts. WIPO did pass new amendments to the Berne Convention of 1886, affording more protection to sound recordings, "copyright management information" (to prevent plagiarism), and copy-protection technologies (to prevent piracy), but the database-protection issue was laid to rest—for now.

It's expected that database protection and other intellectual property issues—including the implementation of the new WIPO copyright rules—will be among the hottest debated online sociopolitical issues for some time.

FIVE | THE CODE OF

ONLINE
CONDUCT?

Learning Netiquette, Fighting Spam,
Recognizing Spoof Email,
Dealing with Hackers and Crackers,
Treating Viruses, Spotting Scams,
and Ensuring Equality

"On the Internet nobody knows you're a dog, but they sure know if
you're a son of a bitch."

STEVE CISLER, APPLE COMPUTER

Responsibility is really what this book is about. Indeed, all the legislation in the world, in all the jurisdictions that ever existed, wouldn't
be able to reliably control behavior on the Net. That's up to individual users. But it's not our intent to dictate appropriate behavior here,
or even to suggest what *might* be appropriate for you. Rather, we
offer our observations of that which has become accepted as convention by those using the various new media. We look at specific problems and subject areas and offer at least one viewpoint (and hopefully

more) for you to base your own judgment on. We start with the belief that all rights stem from responsibility, and responsible behavior is rewarded with desirable results.

The previous chapters have shown how a global medium presents challenges unlike anything we've had to deal with before. In the new many-to-many medium, there's reason for great optimism. The twofold challenge is for us to create community standards for this new global netspace and make those standards enforceable by rewarding good behavior rather than by punishing bad (or perhaps some combination of both). If the Internet-user community can do this, the Net will be better able to reach its potential to empower us all, impacting society as a whole in positive ways. Some of that potential impact will be obvious as you read this chapter.

In order to understand social responsibility issues online, we must first understand that being online means that we're part of a community, much as we are in our physical communities. Unlike our more familiar geographical communities, however, online communities are usually based on affinity or interest.

The Internet is a linked network of networks, or smaller communities, as we've noted, each with its own local standards and "ordinances." Take, for example, America Online, CompuServe, and other service providers that also offer content. They spell out rules for members communicating within their own "gated" limits. They also have conspicuous warnings to users venturing out on the open Internet—warnings that disavow responsibility for what's to be found or experienced out there. Indeed, some even have safeguards to prevent certain individuals (children, for example) from venturing outside without authorization.

The convenience and security of being within such an online community are advantages that make sense for many online customers, especially families. Customers who find such restrictions more of a hindrance than a valued service have many other

Internet service providers to choose from, most of which offer simple access to the Net (rather than edited content within the service itself).

Once out on the Net, users have the option of visiting sites on the World Wide Web, exchanging email, downloading software from FTP sites, or participating in discussions on Usenet newsgroups. Each of these areas of online interaction has its own set of social customs and (usually) unwritten rules, often referred to as "netiquette."

A Brief Guide to Netiquette

Netiquette has evolved over the short history of the Internet through the common experiences of users. Much like the early settlers of the United States, early users of the Internet found that certain behaviors online were disruptive or damaging, and they developed ways to let offenders know of their transgression. These early methods of alerting a user about a breach of proper netiquette included a harsh upbraiding known as a "flame." One flame frequently spawned another, however, and hostile messages between people (who in many cases hadn't met) often escalated into insult contests known as "flame wars." Most Net users these days will tell you that a flame itself is bad netiquette (in addition to being damaging to personal and professional relationships).

How can you learn about such behavioral expectations in advance, so that you can avoid offending others or being flamed? The first thing you should do is observe: watch how others behave in the area of the Net in which you're participating. Take your time before jumping into discussions, and if possible, do some homework to see what transpired in discussions before you got there. You'll find plenty of cues from those who preceded you.

Here are some additional pointers:

• *Remember that we're all human beings.* The fact that the medium is text doesn't mean that those who will read your message don't have feelings. Even though the computer, your tool, separates you from your audience, don't forget that harsh language can be just as hurtful as a slap in the face.

Human nature being what it is, you're more likely to persuade others to see your point if you present your case respectfully, rationally, and without attacking the other's point of view. Abusing others leaves people thinking less of you, and less likely to be your ally when you need them.

It's a good idea to give yourself time to cool down when reacting to something emotional online. There's rarely anything lost by waiting a few minutes to rationally consider things, but there's often a lot to lose by hastily reacting with an angry email or flaming post. Once it's unleashed, your outburst will reach its target in seconds. You might also try the "mom" test mentioned in Chapter 2. If you wouldn't want your mom to read a message you've composed, or want to have it overheard in a crowded room, you might not want to send it as written.

• *Don't blame system administrators.* Occasionally, you may find cause to write to a system administrator about a rule or netiquette violation. While a written complaint sometimes brings action, remember that an administrator (though responsible for enforcing the rules of the community) isn't always able to prevent a user from behaving in an inappropriate manner. If you *do* request help in solving a problem, be courteous; you're more likely to get the help you need if you ask rather than demand.

• *Watch what you say about others.* Whether you're posting in a newsgroup, chatting in a chat room, casually sending email, or filling out a form on the Web, you're doing so in public. It may seem like a personal communication at the time, but there's the potential for millions of people on the Net (including, odds are, some who know you) to see what you've written. For this reason, it's a very good idea to think twice about posting personal information about yourself and others. Think about potential damage that could be done if that information got into the wrong hands. (As you know from earlier chapters, any posting is easily retransmitted!)

- *Be concise.* Short messages have greater impact. It's better to make your point in ten words than in twenty. The longer your message, the fewer people will take the time to read it.

- *Check your spelling.* It's common sense, but it really helps. Your writing is all that some people will ever know of you, so why not make the best possible impression?

- *Use subject lines where appropriate.* The subject line of an email or a Usenet article is intended to enable a person with a limited amount of time to decide whether or not to read your words. You do yourself and others a service by titling appropriately. Some email programs and newsgroups truncate titles at forty characters, so remember to keep them short.

- *Remember your audience.* When posting to a newsgroup, it's considered very poor form to be off topic, or to address a global audience about a local issue. Consider the place you're communicating in and the audience you're communicating with, and tailor your message appropriately. And think of newsgroups as fellow conversationalists. You wouldn't normally walk up to a group of people and butt into their conversation. You'd listen first, then offer something when the time was right, after hearing what was being discussed.

• *Use humor and sarcasm carefully.* Just how important are body language and voice inflection in our communication? Some of us find out for the first time in online messages that were meant to be funny but are taken the wrong way. In written communication, subtle humor is very difficult to convey (or pick up on), especially when the writer and reader aren't very familiar with each other.

One of the ways the Net community has attempted to compensate for this lack of visual and audio cues is through the use of "emoticons." These are pictures created with standard text letters and punctuation, which if turned clockwise ninety degrees appear to be expressions. (See the sidebar below for examples.) While these symbols can be helpful, they can also be distracting and annoying. We advise you to use them judiciously.

• *Don't repost the same message.* Avoid posting a message to more than one newsgroup unless you're sure what you have to say is appropriate for that broader audience. If you do wish to post to multiple newsgroups, specify all the groups on a single copy of the message rather than posting to each separately. This reduces network clutter and allows those who subscribe to more than one of the targeted groups to see the message only once instead of repeatedly.

Similarly, if you subscribe to a mailing list and want to respond to someone's position, it's best to quote only the relevant parts of the message you're responding to, rather than reposting someone's long dissertation only to state, "I agree," at the end. An even better way to respond, whether in newsgroups or mailing lists, is to summarize the statement in question. You'll be communicating more effectively, and less annoyingly, to those who've already read the text in question.

- *Strip headers and credit sources.* Another good practice is to strip the headers off any messages you quote, because they often contain personal information the sender wouldn't wish broadcast out on the Net. Furthermore, they frequently contain gobbledy-gook that others simply wouldn't want to wade through. But stripping identifying headers doesn't mean claiming quoted material as your own. It's good practice to credit your sources when quoting someone else's words or content.

- *Check headers before follow-up.* Make sure that your responses go to the right place. Some news software provides that follow-ups to an article must go to a specific set of newsgroups, possibly different from those to which the original article was sent. Similarly, some mailing lists automatically send messages back to the entire list when you hit the REPLY button. Others send the message back only to the originator of the message. It's a good idea to double-check where your message is heading before hitting SEND.

- *Watch out for copyrighted material.* Reposting something you saw online is a fairly safe endeavor; however, it's never without risk to assume that something is in the public domain. Look for the copyright notice or symbol (which should be present whenever a copyrighted work appears) before reposting. And remember that you're publishing in a potentially public place, so you should avoid posting trade secrets.

- *Tolerate mistakes.* Time and time again on Usenet or in mailing lists, someone will correct the spelling or grammar of a contributor, triggering the analysis and correction of dozens of messages for weeks at a time. This isn't productive behavior, often hurts feelings, and doesn't take into consideration the fact that people have varying language skills. Some have learned English as a second language; others suffer dyslexia or another condition that makes it difficult to type perfectly. Tolerance pays off in better understanding all around.

- *Be aware of line-length and nonstandard-character limitations.* Based on the modem terminal programs that were widely used during the Net's early days, an eighty-character line length became the de facto standard for online communication. These terminal programs, capable of transmitting text only (also referred to as ASCII text), are still widely used today. When you post a document that has lines longer than eighty characters, these programs don't automatically wrap the text, as you'd expect from a word processor. Because the resulting broken lines and concatenated paragraphs are difficult to follow, many potential readers will be discouraged from reading your message. Therefore, even if your email program allows more flexibility in line length and text format, it's a good idea to stick with the traditional unless it's absolutely necessary that you do otherwise.

- *Don't overdo your signature.* Many email and news programs include a feature that allows for the automatic addition of what's called the "signature." Your signature is information, custom-provided by you, that allows others to easily identify and respond to you. The fundamental guideline on signatures is to keep them short. A signature longer than the message itself is considered bad netiquette. Use your signature to help people locate you, not to tell your life story. It should include your return email address and any other personal contact data you don't mind having available in public. Four lines is a good maximum to shoot for.

Online Symbology

If you're new to online communication, you'll find the following list of emoticons and acronyms useful in sending/reading email and visiting chat rooms. These symbols are frequently used on the Net. As an example, it's customary to wave (::hi::) and grin (:D) when entering a chat room. You can also create your own choreographic pictures by combining words with these symbols: ("walking over to Cyberguy, giving him a big hug {{ }}").

Typing in all caps is considered shouting and should be reserved for occasions when a loud voice is absolutely necessary.

To see the intended effect of the following symbols, tilt the page clockwise ninety degrees.

:) = smile	---<---@ = a rose
:D = smile/laugh/grin	LOL = laughing out loud
:* = kiss	OTF = on the floor (laughing)
;) = wink	ROTF = rolling on the floor
:: = wave	ROFLWTIME = rolling on floor
:X = my lips are sealed	with tears in my eyes
:P = sticking out my tongue	AFK = away from keyboard
{} = hug	BAK = back at keyboard
:(= frown	BRB = be right back
:'(= crying	TTFN = ta-ta for now!
O:) = angel	WB = welcome back
}:> = devil	JK = just kidding
:O = amazed	BTW = by the way
:I = bored	GMTA = great minds think alike
:> = devilish grin	CUL8R = see you later
B) = wearing my shades	WTG = way to go

Had Enough Spam?

Over the years of the Net's development, the Hormel Foods Corporation has allowed its valuable trademark for the product named Spam to be appropriated by Internet users to refer to automatically transmitted junk email (although Hormel is now beginning to act in defense of the name). We've all seen this kind of email, offering get-rich-quick schemes, great deals on new software technology, and packages containing a program that generates this very kind of email. There are many parallels between traditional junk mail and this Net-based version, but there are just as many dissimilarities. The digital version of junk mail presents its own set of problems and potential solutions.

Probably we can all recall having received at least one unsolicited offer in both our regular mailbox and our email box—an offer describing something we supposedly really want or need. Still, the ratio of ten or more useless items to one we're really interested in—a common ratio for those who spend much time on the Net—is unacceptable to most of us.

The differences between junk mail in your mailbox and in your email box include the following:

1. It usually takes longer to determine whether you're really interested in electronic messages. You have to open each message and read at least a portion to determine whether it's of interest.

2. Since junk messages aren't regulated as traditional interstate mail is, there's a higher percentage of fraud present.

3. While a letter can sit in the mailbox for days at no cost to the recipient, many users must pay for the storage of messages on their email servers.

4. Since there's virtually no incremental cost (the equivalent of postage) in adding hundreds of thousands of messages electronically, there's no *dis*incentive to spammers to blanket as many addresses as they can get.

Contrary to what many people fear, the large volume of junk email to be found in distribution today isn't "clogging" the Net. (Text requires very little bandwidth.) Unsolicited messages are, however, clogging people's mail servers and wasting their time, and therefore they're certainly cause for concern.

Some of the attempted solutions to spamming are as bad as (or worse than) the problem they attempt to address. One such method is known as "mail-bombing"—a technique similar to spamming, but in reverse. Whereas spamming involves a single identical message going from one location to many, mail-bombing is the sending of many messages from as many locations as possible to a single location (the spammer). When mail-bombing—a technique considered un-ethical by many—achieves its objectives, it effectively shuts down the targeted email account. It usually doesn't work, however, because flagrant spammers often hide behind forged headers.

Other techniques that are considered poor choices (and in some circumstances are illegal) include "phone-flooding" and "fax-bombing." In phone-flooding, frustrated junk email recipients program their modem to dial the toll-free number of the spammer repeatedly, preventing any other calls from getting through. (This solution is rarely attempted, primarily because spammers don't give out toll-free numbers much these days.) Fax-bombing, as the name implies, is a similar practice: recipients flood the fax machine of the spammer, giving him or her a taste of spamming practices. The nearby sidebar includes several ways to combat this problem that are likely to yield better results.

Ten Ways to Fight Junk Email

I. Send a reply to each person or organization that sends you unwanted messages, asking the sender to refrain from trans-mitting unsolicited junk mail around the Internet. Since most legitimate businesses would rather build goodwill with potential customers than alienate them, this will have a positive effect at least some of the time. However, it's not likely to impress the less-than-legitimate businesses that contribute to junk email.

II. Pay a visit to *http://kenjen.com/nospam/,* a legitimate site that offers junk emailers a chance to purge their lists of people who don't wish to receive unsolicited email. Of course, there's no guarantee that a spammer will check this list before launching a mailing. This site also has information about reporting junk email and Net abuse.

III. File a complaint. Let's say you've politely requested that you be removed from a particular list but find that you're still receiving unwanted messages. The next step is a politely worded message to the spammer's service provider—if in fact you can determine who that is. For example, send your complaint to: *postmaster@*[host.]*site.domain* (for example, *postmaster@aol.com*). Here are some of the popular service providers' reporting addresses:

- *America Online: abuse@aol.com, tosemail1@aol.com, then tosemail2@aol.com (tos means "terms of service")*
- *CompuServe: postmaster@compuserve.com or ecgintern@csi.compuserve.com*
- *Prodigy: mailadm@prodigy.com or postmaster@prodigy.com*
- *AT&T WorldNet: abuse@worldnet.att.net*
- *Earthlink: spam@earthlink.net or abuse@earthlink.net*
- *Netcom: abuse@netcom.com*

AOL has created a Preferred Mail option (keyword: preferredmail) that works much like the Web site listed in the second suggestion above: it gives responsible spammers a way to identify unwilling recipients and remove them from their list. It's a good idea to remember that no service provider can monitor all of its many users, but if a provider receives a number of complaints about the same abuse, it may be able to take action in the future.

IV. If the problem continues, you can write politely but more firmly to the spammer's service provider, explaining that you don't appreciate the unsolicited or fraudulent mail. Ask that the provider take disciplinary action. Include the complete original spam with all header information. Simply copy it into your message (but don't forget to remove cc's and bcc's, or you'll be guilty of sending junk messages yourself).

V. Report suspicious or annoying messages to your own service provider. Often these ISP businesses band together to locate and stop fraudulent activity that affects their user-bases.

VI. Filter spam using your own email software. An excellent, detailed explanation of how to do this with Eudora is found at *http://wso.williams.edu/~eudora/eudora–3–0 -spam-filter.html.* AOL members should go to keyword: *preferredmail.* Another option is "The Spam Bouncer" at *http://www.best.com/~ariel/nospam/.*

VII. Visit the Get That Spammer! Web site: *http://kryten.eng.monash.edu.au/gspam.html.* This site has tools for tracing the email addresses of spammers. Once you've identified them, you can use the InterNIC WHOIS tool (*http://rs.internic.net/cgi-bin/whois*) to identify administrative (or other appropriate) contacts for their service providers.

VIII. Report offenders to the appropriate newsgroups, after checking to see that the abuse hasn't already appeared in others' posts. Post a copy of the message, with headers, subject line,

and body intact, to the following Usenet newsgroup:
news.admin.net-abuse.sightings. Then send follow-ups to:
  • *news.admin.net-abuse.email (for junk email you received)*
  • *news.admin.net-abuse.usenet (for junk messages posted to newsgroups)*

IX. Use encrypted signatures (employing Pretty Good Privacy or other encryption technologies) in exchanging email messages, guaranteeing authentication. You'll then be sure that messages are from the sender they purport to be from and that the content is received unchanged.

X. If you have good reason to believe a crime has been committed in the electronic communication process, contact your national enforcement agency. In the United States, that agency is:

FBI National Computer Crimes Squad
Washington, D.C.
(202) 324-9164

U.S. citizens also have the National Fraud Information Center at their disposal: *http://www.fraud.org/*.

Forged Email or "Spoofing"

Email spoofing occurs when a user receives email appearing to have originated from one source when it actually was sent from another. Email spoofing can be an attempt to trick you into making a damaging statement or releasing sensitive information (such as a password). You might, for example, receive a message purporting to be from your system administrator requesting you to change your password, threatening suspension of your account if you don't comply. You might even be asked for your password outright. These kinds of messages are rarely the real thing. Most service providers publish a policy that warns you to look for fraudulent attempts to get you to divulge private information. In most cases, they also publish instructions on how to report these incidents.

It's easy for savvy users to spoof email, because Simple Mail Transfer Protocol (SMTP) lacks authentication of the sort available with encryption. This common Internet mail protocol allows virtually anyone to connect to the SMTP port on a service provider's site and issue commands to send email that appears to be from the address of the transgressor's choice—either an actual user's address or a fictitious address formatted correctly. The former works well for spoofers, while spammers prefer the latter (because replies are undeliverable). Other tricks, such as modifying a Web-browser interface, give spoofers additional means of creating communications that aren't what they seem to be.

An Update
by Stanton McCandlish, *mech@eff.org*

As of January 1996, some spamming advertisers, apparently in response to megabytes of hate mail, have taken to putting the character string {B} in the subject lines of their messages, to indicate that the messages are bulk-class mail. The presence of this string enables one to filter out {B}-bearing messages with any email filter capable of examining message subject headers and disposing of messages that fit the criterion.

It should be noted that while this is a nice gesture, it's unlikely to be a sufficient solution. Aside from the fact that it goes against the grain of current Internet standards, in which urgency is indicated in a particular header (which already supports a "bulk" category!), many users (1) cannot filter their mail, and/or (2) still have to pay for filtered-out mail. As usual, those who are currently

spamming would do well to learn some netiquette and take up
www-based advertising instead of bombarding people's email
boxes by the thousands.

Hacking and Cracking

It's mid-evening in a quiet suburban neighborhood. Alexander, age
nineteen, is sitting at his computer terminal, typing tentatively in an
arcane computer-programming language. When he finally hits the
ENTER key, he sees a string of characters on the screen that tell him he's
in! Now that he's gotten past the security of the system or network he's
been trying to get into, the "packet sniffer" program he's using is able
to detect the content of email messages, observe people engaged in
gaming, and—the grand prize—watch someone logging on. In that
latter activity, Alexander can see the user's ID and password, and these
are his keys to enter the system as that user, with all his actions done in
that user's name. Should that user be an administrator or executive of
the network, our young subject may be able to acquire secret information about other users and other networks, or—if he's savvy enough—
even bring that particular system to a dead halt.

This is an example of common Internet "cracking"—an activity
that's always inappropriate and sometimes, depending on the intent,
the damage done, and the jurisdiction involved, also illegal. The subject of "cracking"—and its close sibling, hacking—remains controversial, with questions of ethics and intentionality at the forefront.

Let's define the terms *hacking* and *cracking,* since they're crucial to
this discussion. Both terms refer to the unauthorized (and potentially
harmful) access of systems and data. The distinction between the two
lies in intent. Over the years, a subset of those individuals engaged in
hacking have claimed that their intentions are merely to point out
the weaknesses that exist in a system or network; their aim is to do a

valuable service rather than harm users and operators. The term that's sprung up for unauthorized activity done with this aim is *cracking*. Depending on the process used, the nature of the targeted system, and the jurisdiction(s) in which the actions took place, cracking can be illegal. At the very least, crackers are skating on thin ethical ice.

Confusingly, *hacking* can also mean "consummate programming or other work," and *cracking* can mean "disabling copy protection for software piracy purposes" (itself an ethically questionable activity). In their more common usage, however, these terms distinguish those who are performing a useful, benevolent service to the software industry from those whose purpose is malicious or destructive (or just illegal). Over the past few years, a strong movement has developed in the hacker community to repair their image as mischief-makers or criminals. Hackers are, in many cases, consultants who work with software developers to ensure that the programs you buy are secure from crackers, whom these hackers identify as the group actually doing misdeeds!

Some of the legal and ethical issues surrounding the civil liberties that hackers and crackers bring to light are examined in the following essay by EFF co-founder Mitch Kapor:

Civil Liberties in Cyberspace:
When Does Hacking Turn from an
Exercise of Civil Liberties into Crime?

by Mitchell Kapor, EFF co-founder (comments excerpted from an article published in *Scientific American,* September 1991)

On March 1, 1990, the U.S. Secret Service raided the offices of Steve Jackson, an entrepreneurial publisher in Austin, Texas. Carrying a search warrant, the authorities confiscated computer hardware and software, the drafts of his about-to-be-released book, and many business records of his company, Steve Jackson Games. They also seized the electronic bulletin-board system used by the publisher to communicate with customers and writers, thereby seizing all the private electronic mail on the system.

The Secret Service held some of the equipment and material for months, refusing to discuss their reasons for the raid. The publisher was forced to reconstruct his book from old manuscripts, to delay filling orders for it, and to lay off half his staff. When the warrant application was finally unsealed months later, it confirmed that the publisher was never suspected of any crime.

Steve Jackson's legal difficulties are symptomatic of a widespread problem. During the past several years, dozens of individuals have been the subject of similar searches and seizures. In any other context, this warrant might never have been issued. By many interpretations, it disregarded the First and Fourth Amendments to the U.S. Constitution, as well as several existing privacy laws. But the government proceeded as if civil liberties did not apply. In this case, the government was investigating a new kind of crime—computer crime.

The circumstances vary, but a disproportionate number of cases share a common thread: the serious misunderstanding of computer-based communication and its implications for civil liberties. We now face the task of adapting our legal institutions and societal expectations to the cultural phenomena that even now are springing up from communications technology.

Our society has made a commitment to openness and to free communication. But if our legal and social institutions fail to adapt to new technology, basic access to the global electronic media could be seen as a privilege, granted to those who play by the strictest rules, rather than as a right held by anyone who needs to communicate. To assure that these freedoms are not compromised, a group of computer experts, including myself, founded the Electronic Frontier Foundation (EFF) in 1990. In many respects, it was odd that Steve Jackson Games got caught up in a computer crime investigation at all. The company publishes a popular, award-winning series of fantasy role-playing games, produced in the form of elaborate rule books. The raid took place only because law enforcement officials misunderstood the technologies—computer bulletin-board systems (BBSs) and online forums—and misread the cultural phenomena that those technologies engender.

Like a growing number of businesses, Steve Jackson Games operated an electronic bulletin board to facilitate contact between players of its games and their authors. Users of this bulletin-board system dialed in via modem from their personal computers to swap strategy tips, learn about game upgrades, exchange electronic mail, and discuss games and other topics.

Law enforcement officers apparently became suspicious when a Steve Jackson Games employee—on his own time and on a BBS he ran from his house—made an innocuous comment about a public-domain protocol for transferring computer files called Kermit. In addition, officials claimed that at one time the employee had had on an electronic bulletin board a copy of Phrack, a widely disseminated electronic publication that included information they believed to have been stolen from a BellSouth computer. The law enforcement officials interpreted these facts as unusual enough to justify not only a search and seizure at the employee's residence but also the search of Steve Jackson Games and the seizure of enough equipment to disrupt the business seriously. Among the items confiscated were all the hard copies and electronically stored copies of the manuscript of a rule book for a role-playing game called GURPS Cyberpunk, in which inhabitants of so-called cyberspace invade corporate and government computer systems and steal sensitive data. Law enforcement agents regarded the book, in the words of one, as "a handbook for computer crime."

A basic knowledge of the kinds of computer intrusion that are technically possible would have enabled the agents to see that GURPS Cyberpunk was nothing more than a science fiction creation and that Kermit was simply a legal, frequently used computer program. Unfortunately, the agents assigned to investigate computer crime did not know what—if anything—was evidence of criminal activity. Therefore, they intruded on a small business without a reasonable basis for believing that a crime had been committed and conducted a search and seizure without looking for "particular" evidence, in violation of the Fourth Amendment of the Constitution.

Searches and seizures of such computer systems affect the rights of not only their owners and operators but also the users of those systems. Although most BBS users have never been in the same room with the actual computer that carries their postings, they legitimately expect their electronic mail to be private and their lawful associations to be protected.

The community of bulletin-board users and computer networkers may be small, but precedents must be understood in a greater context. As forums for debate and information exchange, computer-based bulletin boards and conferencing systems support some of the most vigorous exercise of the First Amendment freedoms of expression and association that this country has ever seen. Moreover, they are evolving rapidly into large-scale public information and communications utilities. These utilities will probably converge into a digital national public network that will connect nearly all homes and businesses in the United States.

This network will serve as a main conduit for commerce, learning, education and entertainment in our society, distributing images and video signals as well as text and voice. Much of the content of this network will be private messages serving as "virtual" town halls, village greens, and coffeehouses, where people post their ideas in public or semipublic forums. Yet there is a common perception that a defense of electronic civil liberties is somehow opposed to legitimate concerns about the prevention of computer crime. The conflict arises, in part, because the popular hysteria about the technically sophisticated youths known as hackers has drowned out reasonable discussion. Perhaps inspired by the popular movie *WarGames,* the general public began in the 1980s to perceive computer hackers as threats to the safety of this country's vital computer systems. But the image of hackers as malevolent is purchased at the price of ignoring the underlying reality—the typical teenage hacker is simply tempted by the prospect of exploring forbidden territory. Some are among our best and brightest technological talents: hackers of the 1960s and 1970s, for example, were so driven by their desire to master, understand, and produce new hardware and software that they went on to start companies called Apple, Microsoft, and Lotus.

How do we resolve this conflict? One solution is ensure that our scheme of civil and criminal laws provides sanctions in proportion to the offenses. A system in which an exploratory hacker receives more time in jail than a defendant convicted of assault violates our sense of justice. Our legal tradition historically has shown itself capable of making subtle and not-so-subtle distinctions among criminal offenses. There are, of course, real threats to network and system security. The qualities that make the ideal network valuable—its popularity, its uniform commands, its ability to handle financial transactions, and its international access—also make it vulnerable to a variety of abuses and accidents. It is certainly proper to hold hackers accountable for their offenses, but that accountability should never entail denying defendants the safeguards of the Bill of Rights, including the rights to free expression and association and to freedom from unreasonable searches and seizures.

We need statutory schemes that address the acts of true computer criminals (such as those who have created the growing problem of toll and credit-card fraud) while distinguishing between those criminals and hackers whose acts are most analogous to noncriminal trespass. And we need educated law enforcement officials who will be able to recognize and focus their efforts on the real threats.

The question then arises: How do we help our institutions, and perceptions, adapt? The first step is to articulate the kinds of values we want to see protected in the electronic society we are now shaping and to make an agenda for preserving the civil liberties that are central to that society. Then we can draw on the appropriate legal traditions that guide other media. The late Ithiel de Sola Pool argued in his influential book *Technologies of Freedom* that the medium of digital communications is heir to several traditions of control: the press, the common carrier, and the broadcast media.

The freedom of the press to print and distribute is explicitly guaranteed by the First Amendment. This freedom is somewhat limited, particularly by laws governing obscenity and defamation, but the thrust of First Amendment law, especially in this century, prevents the government from imposing "prior restraint" on publications. Like the railroad networks, the telephone networks follow common-carrier principles—they do not impose content restrictions on the "cargo" they carry. It would be unthinkable for the telephone company to monitor our calls routinely or cut off conversations because the subject matter was deemed offensive. Meanwhile, the highly regulated broadcast media are grounded in the idea, arguably mistaken, that spectrum scarcity and the pervasiveness of the broadcast media warrant government allocation and control of access to broadcast frequencies (and some control of content). Access to this technology is open to any consumer who can purchase a radio or television set, but it is nowhere near as open for information producers.

Networks as they now operate contain elements of publishers, broadcasters, bookstores, and telephones, but no one model fits. This hybrid demands new thinking or at least a new application of the old legal principles. As hybrids, computer networks also have some features that are unique among the communications media. For example, most conversations on bulletin boards, chat lines, and conferencing systems are both public and private at once. The electronic communicator speaks to a group of individuals, only some of whom are known personally, in a discussion that may last for days or months.

But the dissemination is controlled, because the membership is limited to the handful of people who are in the virtual room, paying attention. Yet the result may also be "published"—an archival textual or voice record can be automatically preserved, and newcomers can read the backlog. Some people tend to equate online discussions with party (or party-line) conversations, whereas others compare them to newspapers and still others think of citizens band radio.

Freedom of speech on networks will be promoted by limiting content-based regulations and by promoting competition among providers of network services. The first is necessary because governments will be tempted to restrict the content of any information service they subsidize or regulate. The second is necessary because market competition is the most efficient means of ensuring that needs of network users will be met.

All electronic "publishers" should be allowed equal access to networks. Ultimately, there could be hundreds of thousands of these information providers, as there are hundreds of thousands of print publishers today. As "nodes," they will be considered the conveners of the environments within which online assembly takes place. None of the old definitions will suffice for this role. For example, to safeguard the potential of free and open inquiry, it is desirable to preserve each electronic publisher's control over the general flow and direction of material under his or her imprimatur, in effect, to give the "sysop," or system operator, the prerogatives and protections of a publisher.

But it is unreasonable to expect the sysop of a node to review every message or to hold the sysop to a publisher's standard of libel. Message traffic on many individually owned services is already too great for the sysop to review. We can only expect the trend to grow. Nor is it appropriate to compare nodes to broadcasters (an analogy likely to lead to licensing and content-based regulation). Unlike the broadcast media, nodes do not dominate the shared resource of a public community, and they are not a pervasive medium. To take part in a controversial discussion, a user must actively seek entry into the appropriate node, usually with a subscription and a password.

Anyone who objects to the content of a node can find hundreds of other systems where they might articulate their ideas more freely. The danger is if choice is somehow restricted: if all computer networks in the country are restrained from allowing discussion on particular subjects or if a publicly sponsored computer network limits discussion. This is not to say that freedom-of-speech principles ought to protect all electronic communications. Exceptional cases, such as the BBS used primarily to traffic in stolen long-distance access codes or credit-card numbers, will always arise and pose problems of civil and criminal liability. We know that electronic freedom of speech, whether in public or private systems, cannot be absolute. In face-to-face conversation and printed matter today, it is commonly agreed that freedom of speech does not cover the communications inherent in criminal conspiracy, fraud, libel, incitement to lawless action, and copyright infringement. If there are to be limits on electronic freedom of speech, what precisely should those limits be? One answer to this question is the U.S. Supreme Court's 1969 decision in *Brandenburg* v. *Ohio*. The court ruled that no speech should be subject to prior restraint or criminal prosecution unless it is intended to incite and is likely to cause imminent lawless action.

In general, little speech or publication falls outside the protections of the *Brandenburg* case, since most people are able to reflect before acting on a written or spoken suggestion. As in traditional media, any online messages should not be the basis of criminal prosecution unless the *Brandenburg* standard is met. Other helpful precedents include cases relating to defamation and copyright infringement. Free speech does not mean one can damage a reputation or appropriate a copyrighted work without being called to account for it. And it probably does not mean that one can release a virus across the network in order to "send a message" to network subscribers. Although the distinction is trickier than it may first appear, the release of a destructive program, such as a virus, may be better analyzed as an act rather than as speech.

Following freedom of speech on our action agenda is freedom from unreasonable searches and seizures. The Steve Jackson case was one of many cases in which computer equipment and disks were seized and held sometimes for months—often without a specific charge being filed. Even when only a few files were relevant to an investigation, entire computer systems, including printers, have been removed with their hundreds of files intact.

Such nonspecific seizures and searches of computer data allow "rummaging," in which officials browse through private files in search of incriminating evidence. In addition to violating the Fourth Amendment requirement that searches and seizures be "particular," these searches often run afoul of the Electronic Communications Privacy Act of 1986. This act prohibits the government from seizing or intercepting electronic communications without proper authorization. They also contravene the Privacy Protection Act of 1980, which prohibits the government from searching the offices of publishers for documents, including materials that are electronically stored.

We can expect that law enforcement agencies and civil libertarians will agree over time about the need to establish procedures for searches and seizures of "particular" computer data and hardware. Law enforcement officials will have to adhere to guidelines in the above statutes to achieve Fourth Amendment "particularity" while maximizing the efficiency of their searches. They also will have to be trained to make use of software tools that allow searches for particular files or particular information within files on even the most capacious hard disk or optical storage device.

There is general agreement, for example, that a policy on electronic crime should offer protection for security and privacy on both individual and institutional systems. Defining a measure of damages and setting proportional punishment will require further good-faith deliberations by the community involved with electronic freedoms, including the Federal Bureau of Investigation, the Secret Service, the bar associations, technology groups, telephone companies, and civil libertarians. It will be especially important to represent the damage caused by electronic crime accurately and to leave room for the valuable side of the hacker spirit: the interest in increasing legitimate understanding through exploration.

We hope to see a similar emerging consensus on security issues. Network systems should be designed not only to provide technical solutions to security problems but also to allow system operators to use them without infringing unduly on the rights of users. A security system that depends on wholesale monitoring of traffic, for example, would create more problems than it would solve.

Those parts of a system where damage would do the greatest harm—financial records, electronic mail, military data—should be protected. This involves installing more effective computer security measures, but it also means redefining the legal interpretations of copyright, intellectual property, computer crime, and privacy so that system users are protected against individual criminals and abuses by large institutions. These policies should balance the need for civil liberties against the need for a secure, orderly, protected electronic society.

Why do hackers and crackers go to great lengths to ply their skills, often at great risk and with no monetary objective? The answer may be "because they can." In this account of the famous Kevin Mitnick case, we glimpse a behavioral pathology that may not be uncommon on the new frontier.

The Legend of Kevin Mitnick: A Tragic Timeline

It reads like a contemporary movie script, full of obsession, conspiracy, and intrigue. It's the tale of an unlikely individual who chose to demonstrate his intellect and network skills by breaching the security of telephone and computer systems—not for monetary gain but for bragging rights. According to his attorney, it was an addiction.

The story began to unfold during Kevin's high school years at Monroe High in Los Angeles. Here he learned how to access the Los Angeles Unified School District's main computers, and soon found himself in the company of something of a hacker gang, mostly involved in "phone phreaking" activities, such as taking over directory-assistance lines and rerouting calls. Sometime in 1981, Mr. Mitnick (then seventeen) and some friends managed to talk their way past security guards at Pacific Bell and then somehow acquired a list of priority passwords, lock combinations, and confidential operating manuals. An informant subsequently led authorities to the youthful perpetrators. Mitnick received ninety days in Los Angeles Juvenile Detention Center and one year probation.

In 1982, Mitnick and a partner entered the campus of the University of Southern California, using student computers for hacking. They were subsequently arrested by campus police, but charges were dropped. However, the LAPD did use the evidence to send Mitnick to juvenile prison for six months for breaking his probation.

Scroll forward to 1984, when Mitnick was working for Great American Merchandising, a company operated by a family acquaintance. It was there he began running unauthorized TRW credit checks and calling into PacBell computers. A company executive reported this to the district attorney's office, provoking a search of Mitnick's home and sending Mitnick himself into hiding.

Our antihero resurfaced again in 1985, contacting his former partner (who was then working for Hughes Aircraft in El Segundo, California). Mitnick soon visited Hughes and logged on to a National Security Agency computer from there, causing his old partner to lose his job. At about this time, Mitnick enrolled at Computer Learning Center, Los Angeles, where he met his future wife.

Mitnick avoided trouble until 1987, when the Santa Cruz police were alerted to an invasion of the SCO computer system, tracking its source to the home of Mitnick's girlfriend. She and Mitnick were both arrested, although charges of illegally accessing the SCO system were eventually dropped against her. While in custody, Mitnick wasn't allowed access to telephones, for fear he'd commit crimes from behind bars. His attorney soon plea-bargained the felony down to a misdemeanor, resulting in just three years of probation. The romance between Mitnick and his girlfriend blossomed, and they married during the period that followed.

In 1988, Mitnick and his former partner were enrolled at Pierce College, just north of Los Angeles. It wasn't long until the LAPD was once again alerted to suspicious activities connected with the two, who became targets of another investigation. While that investigation was ongoing, Mitnick applied and was considered for a position at Security Pacific Bank. In a close call for that institution, bank officials were tipped off by the LAPD just before Mitnick was offered a job.

Soon thereafter, Kevin and his associate were expelled from Pierce. With nothing but time on his hands, Mitnick turned to his next target: the NASA Jet Propulsion Laboratory in Pasadena. This computer-cracking case made headlines in the *Los Angeles Times* and was retold in the book *Cyberpunk,* by John Markoff.

When Mitnick once again started using his old partner's workplace—this time, Digital Equipment Corporation—as a home for hacking and cracking, that partner decided to cooperate with the FBI. Soon both Mitnick and his partner were arrested for invading DEC systems and allegedly stealing software. The partner, who was convicted of one felony count, received five years probation and community service, while Mitnick was given a one-year sentence at Lompoc Detention facility, along with psychiatric evaluation. His attorneys successfully convinced authorities that his problem was an irrepressible addiction. Soon thereafter, Mitnick and his wife separated.

His next dive under the radar of authorities came in 1992. While he was employed by a Southern California private investigation firm, and still on probation, the FBI appeared at his place of business to arrest him for alleged break-ins at PacBell. In 1994, the California Department of Motor Vehicles initiated a warrant for his arrest on charges of fraudulently attempting to acquire driver identification.

This is where the story begins to take on new dimensions. Sometime in 1995, Netcom Internet Services of San Jose observed that their system had been cracked—an invasion that compromised the confidentiality of several thousand credit-card numbers

and associated personal user information. They called in the FBI.
(Mitnick is reported to have been in Seattle, Washington, at this
time.)

Around the same time, systems security expert Tsutomu
Shimomura of the San Diego Supercomputer Center discovered
that sensitive files were missing there, and the Whole Earth
'Lectronic Link (WELL), a popular electronic bulletin-board system
in the San Francisco area, discovered that its security had been
breached. The latter breach was found to have taken place at
"root" level, meaning that someone had obtained illicit access to
the system at the highest level of authority. WELL was in jeopardy
of being brought down completely.

Instead of shutting down their system, alarming and inconve-
niencing thousands of users, WELL decided to cooperate with
authorities to help track down the perpetrator. They felt it worth
the risk, since it seemed that only a very few accounts had been
targeted. In one of those accounts, they found an unusually large
number of files stored—and in those files were clues suggesting
that they were the missing files sought by Shimomura in San
Diego.

Shimomura was already working with authorities and volunteers. Now WELL's staff joined the electronic manhunt, which
spanned a two-week period in cyberspace and crossed the United
States. By not shutting down and tipping off the intruder, WELL
was able to track his moves online (a demonstration of how an ISP
can be an upstanding cyber-citizen). Those moves led the manhunt to Raleigh, North Carolina, where the suspect was operating
through a computer modem connected to a cellular telephone.
Shimomura then flew to Raleigh, where he and telephone company technicians, along with federal investigators, used cellular-
frequency scanners to home in on the suspect, whom they had
now identified as Mitnick.

In a dramatic 2:00 A.M. arrest operation, they found Mitnick in possession of twenty thousand stolen credit-card records from Netcom. He and Shimomura, acquainted through their online activities, had never met before face to face.

Now Mitnick, wanted in California for a federal parole violation, was charged with two additional federal crimes: illegal use of a telephone access device (punishable by up to fifteen years in prison and a $250,000 fine) and computer fraud (punishable by up to twenty years in prison and a $250,000 fine).

It's not difficult to see how book and movie deals might surface around this story, but there's more to it than drama and excitement. It has important implications for everyone who uses, serves, or regulates cyberspace. First, virtually all of Mitnick's cracking could have been defeated by strong cryptography—ironically, the very cryptography that's been restricted by the U.S. government. Second, law enforcement can and does have the ability to enforce current laws by following traditional and innovative detection methods, as this case demonstrates.

In the Kevin Mitnick case, it was essential that Netcom, WELL, and the Supercomputer Center cooperate with authorities to put a criminal out of action. Despite the obvious benefits of working to fight such crimes, it took courage for those organizations to step forward. Many organizations—other online service providers and banks, for example—shy away from actions that expose their vulnerabilities to scrutiny in open court. Some, fearing loss of customer confidence and further attacks, even agree to pay blackmail money to criminal crackers.

One possible solution in cases such as these is to offer the victims anonymity—much like that offered to rape victims. That protection might motivate them to come forward. It's important for businesses to remember that the cost of fighting malicious hacking activity is always less than the potential damage from not doing so.

Unfortunately, not all businesses are the innocent victims of solo hackers. They're sometimes victims of competitors who resort to hacking tactics or hire crackers to obtain information or do damage. This is obviously serious criminal activity and should be treated as such by targeted companies and law enforcement. To protect your company in the modern networked environment, it's vital to keep up with programs and procedures designed to thwart the latest cracker techniques. One good place for information about this is the Computer Security Institute in San Francisco; you can visit their Web site at *http://www.gocsi.com/*.

Information Warfare

Individuals may have less to worry about from hackers and crackers than do business owners, especially those who use the public networks to transport sensitive data or whose confidential information can be accessed from those networks. And what about government agencies and public utilities? In the late twentieth century, we're hearing more about the potential threat of "cyber-terrorists" to national infrastructures and defense mechanisms. Are these threats real? And if so, why haven't we already seen much evidence of such activity?

Though not well known, some cases of cyber-terrorism have made news:

- "Logic bombs"(a set of instructions hidden in software that when activated can take control of a computer's programs, or crash an entire system) were used to attack telephone network switches in Denver, Atlanta, and Newark, temporarily knocking out service to tens of thousands of people in those regions.

- Hackers from the Netherlands accessed classified military sites during the Gulf War, acquiring secret data on troop locations, warship movement, and weaponry. According to British sources, the information was offered for sale to Saddam Hussein, who rejected it, suspecting a trap.

- An extortion campaign was waged against British banks based on threats of cracker activity. When the extortionists' demands weren't met, tens of millions of dollars were illegally transferred to Swiss accounts. The perpetrators were never caught.

- Ten million dollars was illegally transferred from Citibank to banks in San Francisco, the Netherlands, Israel, Finland, and Germany. The thieves were reported to be former employees who had set up "back doors" in the system before leaving.

The fact is that the more we depend on computers to run our telecommunications, electrical systems, gas and oil storage, transportation, water supply services, and emergency services, the more we need sensible security procedures that equal or surpass the kinds of protection we afford these utilities in the physical world. These are needed to protect us not only from mischievous hackers and malicious crackers, but from enemies of all kinds, as we approach the age where a true information war is possible.

When asked why we haven't seen more damage thus far, given the capability and reality of systems intrusions like the ones described above, a former FBI computer-security expert answered that partly it's been "pure luck."

Viruses

Another "gift" from the cracker and hacker communities is the computer virus. Like their biological counterparts, computer viruses replicate themselves; transmitted from computer to computer, they contain tiny bits of code that may make your machine behave as if it's ill—or worse, may destroy the drive or microprocessor altogether. The less malevolent strains, such as the Stoned virus, merely display a message (in this case, urging the legalization of marijuana). The more destructive viruses, however, can—and do—wreak havoc with individual computers or entire networks.

With the rise in networked computing and the Internet itself, the problem that began in the eighties has gotten worse. The National Center for Computer Crime Data estimates that businesses subjected to unauthorized entries, such as viruses, lose $550 million yearly. In recognition of the gravity of the threat, the Computer Emergency Response Team was developed—a kind of SWAT team instituted by the U.S. Department of Defense to fight the problem of viral attacks on the Net (see *http://www.cert.org*).

Keeping computers and networks virus-free is essential if there's to be free-flowing information in the digital age. A virus-free environment is accomplished with the aid of virus-protection programs that detect and eliminate viruses (and sometimes fix the damage they've done). Several sources offer information on the latest viruses and what to do about them (see Web links listed at the end of this chapter).

Staying Virus-Free

I. Check your system for viruses regularly, using the freeware, shareware, and commercial antivirus programs that are widely available. You may go for years without ever suffering ill effects from viruses, but if they strike when you have no protection, you could lose everything on your computer/network.

II. Most viruses are still spread through floppy disks, so isolating yourself from online services and the Internet can't protect you. It's a good idea to check for viruses each time you insert a floppy into your drive, as well as whenever you download a file from the Internet. Some users also check each time the system boots up.

III. Because prevention is easier than cure, get the latest virus information on the Internet. Consult the following:

- *Usenet newsgroup: comp.virus*
- *Mailing lists:*

  VIRUS-L is for discussions of viruses and antivirus products. Send email to listserv@lehigh.edu. In the body of the message, include the line "sub virus-l your-name" (without the quote marks).

  VALERT-L is for announcements of new viruses. Send email to listserv@lehigh.edu. In the body of the message, include the line "sub valert-l your-name" (again, without the quotes).

- *FTP site: cert.org in pub/virus-l/docs/. This site contains information about viruses and antivirus products, with pointers to other FTP sites.*
- *FAQ on the World Wide Web: http://www.datafellows.fi/vl-faq.htm#A7*

Online Scams

P. T. Barnum is reputed to have said, "There's a sucker born every minute." He didn't know about the Internet, or he might have said there are *dozens* born every minute! Unfortunately, the unscrupulous have gleefully seized their chance to separate gullible individuals from their time and money (by presenting misleading information) on the global Net. This doesn't mean that it's unsafe or unwise to transact business online; it just means that certain precautions should be taken, as in any other medium of communication.

Fraud

One example of online commerce that's become big business is the sale of stocks and securities. How often have you heard or read claims about the availability of stock in "the next Microsoft," or about an investment that's a "guaranteed winner"? Well, you can see those same "yellow-flag" claims on the Net, in teasers designed to hook potential buyers online. Statements such as these are what regulatory and enforcement personnel look for when they attempt to bust scam artists. NASD Regulation, Inc. (The NASD stands for National Association of Securities Dealers) is getting ready to launch a search engine that will poll the chat rooms and bulletin boards where shady stock deals are sometimes made, looking for these key phrases and more. The stock-fraud search engine will then help consumers to verify the reputation of brokers they're considering doing business with—an example of how the same medium that enables new kinds of fraudulent activity also provides the tools to prevent and combat those activities.

The Federal Trade Commission is also spending more time online in efforts to weed out Web businesses whose offers seem too good to be true, and in fact are just that. If you believe that you're involved in a case of online fraud, a good place to learn about your options is the National Fraud Information Center: *http://www.fraud.org/*.

Hoaxes

A close relative of fraud is the online hoax. Generally (but not always) less serious than fraud, hoaxes proliferate in many forms, supplanting harassment as the prevalent variety of online mischief. A hoax may be something as minor as a small bending of the truth in an email message, or it may be as vast as an entire Web site set up to promulgate a falsehood. The intent of hoaxes varies, from simply playing a joke, to defrauding someone out of money or other resources, to serious societal damage. How one views the ethics of the spreading of a hoax is a subjective matter, but most of us would certainly like to know when someone is trying to "put one over on us."

Chain Letters

Some of the most widespread hoaxes that have swept the Net in years past aren't of the pass-something-false-off-as-true variety. More akin to the chain letter, these hoaxes include the "free cookie recipe" story (see below) and what has become a major urban legend, the tale of young Craig Shergold, an English boy who suffered from a supposedly terminal brain tumor. If you've been online for any length of time, you've probably received a letter about Craig. People who forward such letters to others are generally well meaning; they've simply fallen prey to a wasteful prank, a prank that is resurrected with each wave of new Internet users.

As with many legends, the story of Craig Shergold had its basis in fact. Craig was ill in 1989, and with the help of the Make-a-Wish Foundation (and the Internet) was able to get the word out that he wanted to get into the *Guinness Book of Records* for receiving the greatest number of get-well cards. This goal, it turns out, was reached well before the email was widespread: with sixteen million cards received by 1990, he made it into the *Guinness Book* hands down. And there's even better news: the operation to remove the tumor was successful, and Craig has recovered.

The bad news is that various postal services and the Make-a-Wish Foundation are still suffering from the original mailing and its offspring (which came a couple of years later, requesting business cards in place of get-well cards). "Craig said he wishes he could have another wish so he could wish for all this to stop," said

Christy Chappelear, spokeswoman for Children's Wish Foundation International.

Sympathy is the emotional key to this sort of hoax; it explains why busy people who would never consider responding to a chain letter manage to find the time to gather business cards and forward a letter to a dozen friends. Although the Craig Shergold endeavor quickly became a nuisance, the persistence of his story demonstrates how the Net extends the positive as well as the negative aspects of human nature.

While sympathy and good intentions lie behind some hoaxes, others are motivated by harsher emotions. Consider the following message, which—like Craig Shergold's story—has proliferated wildly on the Internet.

Subject: Free Cookies

This message is sent to you with the hope you will forward it to EVERYONE you have ever even seen the e-mail address of. In the spirit of the originator, please feel free to post it anywhere and everywhere.

Okay, everyone … a true story of justice in the good old U.S. of A. Thought y'all might enjoy this; if nothing else, it shows Internet justice, if it can be called that.

My daughter & I had just finished a salad at Neiman-Marcus Cafe in Dallas & decided to have a small dessert. Because our family are such cookie lovers, we decided to try the "Neiman-Marcus Cookie". It was so excellent that I asked if they'd give me the recipe and they said with a small frown, "I'm afraid not." Well, I said, would you let me buy the recipe? With a cute smile, she said, "Yes." I asked how much, and she responded, "Two fifty." I said with approval to just add it to my tab.

Thirty days later, I received my VISA statement from Neiman-Marcus and it was $285.00. I looked again and I remembered I had only spent $9.95 for two salads and about $20.00 for a scarf. As I glanced at the bottom of the statement, it said, "Cookie Recipe—$250.00." Boy, was I upset!! I called Neiman's

Accounting Department and told them the waitress had said "two fifty" and I did not realize she meant $250.00 for a cookie recipe.

I asked them to take back the recipe and reduce my bill and they said they were sorry, but because all the recipes were this expensive so not just everyone could duplicate any of our bakery recipes . . . the bill would stand.

I waited, thinking of how I could get even or even try and get any of my money back.

I just said, "Okay, you folks got my $250.00 and now I'm going to have $250.00 worth of fun." I told her that I was going to see to it that every cookie lover will have a $250.00 cookie recipe from Neiman-Marcus for nothing. She replied, "I wish you wouldn't do this." I said, "I'm sorry, but this is the only way I feel I could get even," and I will.

So, here it is, and please pass it to someone else or run a few copies. . . . I paid for it; now you can have it for free. Have fun!!! This is not a joke; this is a true story. That's it. Please, pass it along to everyone you know, single people, mailing lists, etc . . .

Ride free, citizen!

(Note: The recipe included here was never tried by any of us at EFF, and its authenticity is not verified.)

How *Not* to Be an Internet Hoax Victim

1. Know your source. If you receive email from someone you don't know asking for urgent action, be skeptical. The same goes for posts on newsgroups, bulletin boards, and in chat rooms. Try to verify the identity of the sender by PGP or some other secure method. If you're not sure of the authorship, don't resend the message. Often the identity of a hoaxer is forged, so if you can't verify a message by communicating with the sender, don't believe it.

2. If a message tells you to do something that involves a change in your account or asks you to send a file or message

containing sensitive information over the network, *check with someone you know and trust first.* System administrators rarely use email to accomplish sensitive account transactions, and the need for changes and updates that require you to send files is almost nonexistent. Always double-check with a phone call before complying to such requests.

3. Remember that your emotions may be the target of a hoax message. If you receive something inflammatory or sympathy-inducing, sit back and take a deep breath before acting. If you read something that makes you mad, take the time to analyze the message rationally. And remember that you can't be sure who sent the message until you double-check. Forging an identity can be as easy as sitting at someone's desk when he or she is away.

4. Chain letters and pyramid schemes are as fraudulent in cyberspace as they are in the physical world—and in many cases, just as illegal (see *http://www.usps.gov/websites/depart/inspect/chainlet.htm*). If you decide to forward such a message, don't be surprised if you receive hundreds of angry replies.

5. If the calendar happens to say that it's April 1, you'd be well advised to buffer what you read with an extra layer of patience, supplementing that with a sense of humor. Especially on that day, urgent messages from people you don't know should be dealt with carefully.

Fictitious Virus Announcements

Some of the most disturbing online hoaxes revolve around computer viruses. Because viruses are of considerable concern to most people with computers, any news about potential new viruses receives attention and generates action. Sometimes, however, the news you read online isn't news at all; it's a prank.

Watch Out for Warnings!

Here's a message that appeared in email boxes for the first time around November of 1994:

> Here's some important information. Beware of a file called "Good Times." Happy Chanukah everyone, and be careful out there. There's a virus on America Online being sent by email. If you get anything called "Good Times," DON'T read it or download it. It's a virus that will erase your hard drive. Forward this to all your friends. It may help them a lot.

Then, a few months later, this message appeared:

> Thought you might like to know . . .
>
> Apparently, a new computer virus has been engineered by a user of America Online that is unparalleled in its destructive capability. Other, more well-known viruses, such as Stoned, Airwolf, and Michelangelo, pale in comparison to the prospects of this newest creation by a warped mentality.
>
> What makes this virus so terrifying is the fact that no program needs to be exchanged for a new computer to be infected. It can be spread through the existing email systems of the Internet.
>
> Luckily, there is one sure means of detecting what is now known as the "Good Times" virus. It always travels to new computers the same way—in a text email message with the subject line reading simply "Good Times." Avoiding infection is easy once the file has been received: don't read it. The act of loading the file into the mail server's ASCII buffer causes the "Good Times" mainline program to initialize and execute.
>
> The program is highly intelligent—it will send copies of itself to

everyone whose email address is contained in a received-mail file or a
sent-mail file, if it can find one. It will then proceed to trash the computer it is running on.

   The bottom line here is this: if you receive a file with the subject line
"Good Times," delete it immediately! Do not read it! Rest assured that
whoever's name was on the FROM line was surely struck by the virus.
Warn your friends and local system users of this newest threat to the
Internet! It could save them a lot of time and money.

This sounds like a warning we should have been grateful to
receive. How could Internet users have known it was a hoax?

First, such a virus would have been so dangerous that it would
have been listed at one of the virus-alert sites mentioned earlier in
the chapter. Second, its "pedigree" was unknown. *Any* email that
passes through a chain of recipients should be treated with skepti-
cism. While you (if you received the Good Times warning) may
have known the sender of the message, chances are it had been for-
warded by several people before it got to your friend. And finally, an
email virus isn't possible—at least not in the manner described in
the warning—and a bit of research at the virus-protection Web sites
would have told you that. The closest thing possible to the virus
described would have required a file to be attached to the email
(which would then have had to be downloaded and executed to be
"contagious"). You should of course *never* download a file unless
you're sure of the source—and even then it's a good idea to run
virus-detection software on any file that comes over the Internet.

   Messages such as these about the Good Times virus weren't so
much warnings about viruses as the actual viruses themselves. In
other words, the messages *behaved* like computer viruses: they
consumed bandwidth, disk space, and the valuable time of hundreds of thousands of individuals; and they replicated themselves
all over the network. This was possible only because individuals,

wanting to do a good deed, passed such warnings along without checking the identity or credibility of the originator or the messages, without looking for evidence of the truth of the warnings, and without investigating whether the danger inherent in the messages was technically possible. Had netizens done these things in 1994, they would have discovered the Good Times virus to be a hoax and could have stopped it from wasting people's time and attention.

People find themselves too busy—and sometimes just too lazy—to take these steps; and as a result, every few months, with a new generation of entrants to the Net community coming online, the process repeats itself. We probably haven't seen the end of the Good Times virus hoax, or the story of the dying young boy who wants to get a postcard from *you,* or the recipe from the cookie lady. (Details on these and other hoaxes can be found at *http://ciac.llnl.gov/ciac/CIACHoaxes.html*)

> "The first measure of a free society is not that its government performs the will of the majority. We had that in 1930s Germany and in the South until the '60s. The first measure of a free society is that its government protects the just freedoms of its minorities. The majority is quite capable of protecting itself."
>
> **JIM WARREN,**
> GovAccess

Issues in Online Equality

Although change is happening rapidly, at the time of this writing the majority of Internet inhabitants are white males. These demographics are in stark contrast to the population of the planet (and even of the United States, supposed melting pot of global cultures). It's our hope that the profile of Net users will someday more closely resemble that of the world as a whole, and access will be possible for anyone who wishes it. In the meantime, a variety of factors are affecting how the new media are utilized by women and other marginalized groups. Let's turn to those briefly now.

Gender of U.S. Internet Users

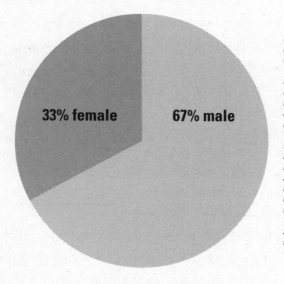

Internet Demographics (courtesy Georgia Institute of Technology) The Net does not currently represent a cross-section of the world population, but trends in every category indicate that it is moving in that direction. These figures represent the latest available data available from a series of surveys conducted by Jim Pitkow and Colleen Kehoe at GVU Center, College of Computing, at the Georgia Institute of Technology, Atlanta, GA 30332-0280. Gender data from O'Reilly & Associates.

Access

Participation in the Internet requires, for most users, a computer, a modem, an extra phone line, and a service provider. Because women and minorities still earn less money than white males, on average, fewer are able to afford access. This in turn prevents the Net from reaching its potential as a means of empowering *everyone*. Public-access programs that make the new technology (and training in that

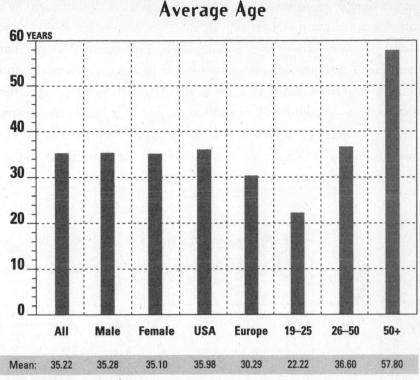

Average Age

Mean:	All	Male	Female	USA	Europe	19–25	26–50	50+
	35.22	35.28	35.10	35.98	30.29	22.22	36.60	57.80

Internet Demographics (courtesy Georgia Institute of Technology)
The Net does not currently represent a cross-section of the world population, but trends in every category indicate that it is moving in that direction. These figures represent the latest available data available from a series of surveys conducted by Jim Pitkow and Colleen Kehoe at GVU Center, College of Computing, at the Georgia Institute of Technology, Atlanta, GA 30332-0280.

technology) available to all individuals—programs offered by public libraries, for example—have the ability to change that.

This disparity in access holds true even among "professional" users—an important point given that most email is sent from the workplace (whether in business or educational settings). White males hold a larger percentage of the technical, academic, and management positions that offer training and subsidized access to online communication, and they make use of that communication with greater frequency and ease.

Disabled individuals join women in the category of those who are not proportionally represented among Internet users. While cost may be a consideration for disabled individuals, they face other obstacles as well—obstacles tied to their limited sight, hearing, or dexterity, for example. There are, however, text-to-voice processors that enable the blind to hear what's being said, and to translate their words into text for communication online. These products are getting better, but they're far from perfected—and they're still fairly costly. Even more costly are custom interfaces for physically impaired individuals—interfaces that allow users to input information in ways that don't require typing.

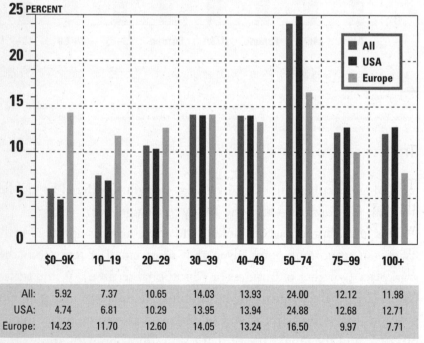

Average Annual Household Income

	$0–9K	10–19	20–29	30–39	40–49	50–74	75–99	100+
All:	5.92	7.37	10.65	14.03	13.93	24.00	12.12	11.98
USA:	4.74	6.81	10.29	13.95	13.94	24.88	12.68	12.71
Europe:	14.23	11.70	12.60	14.05	13.24	16.50	9.97	7.71

Internet Demographics (courtesy Georgia Institute of Technology)
The Net does not currently represent a cross-section of the world population, but trends in every category indicate that it is moving in that direction. These figures represent the latest available data available from a series of surveys conducted by Jim Pitkow and Colleen Kehoe at GVU Center, College of Computing, at the Georgia Institute of Technology, Atlanta, GA 30332-0280.

Furthermore, most Web sites simply are not created with disabled people in mind. Someday, when the Net is considered a utility that all people have the right to participate in, Web pages will be designed to accommodate the disabled just as streets and buildings are planned with them in mind today.

> "Maybe we need a tax credit for the poorest Americans to buy a laptop. Now, maybe that's wrong, maybe that's expensive, maybe we can't do it, but I'll tell you, any signal that we can send to the poorest Americans that says, "We're going into a twenty-first-century, third-wave information age, and so are you, and we want to carry you with us . . ."
>
> **NEWT GINGRICH,**
> speaker of the House of Representatives
> (addressing the House Ways and Means Committee)

Training

The image of the socially isolated computer nerd still prevails, though the stereotype is gradually crumbling. We have to wonder whether that stereotype has deterred women and people of color from entering the computer sciences—a field dominated, like the Internet, by white males—or whether their career choice simply reflects a lack of interest early on. The fact remains that there are fewer African-American, Latino, and women students entering the field than their proportions in the population would suggest. With such a lucrative future ahead of computer graduates, it's a mystery why this is the case. Fortunately, online communication is becoming easier every day, and it doesn't require any real knowledge of how computers work.

Systems *are* becoming easier to operate, but "technophobia" is an obstacle to many users. Computers still call for a lot more savvy than is required to operate a VCR, and this presents a problem for many who are new to the technology. This complexity of use may be the result of who designs the interfaces (engineering-minded males).

Cultural Barriers

"Do you think that having more Web sites which are tailored to your language and culture will make people in your country more willing to use the Web?"

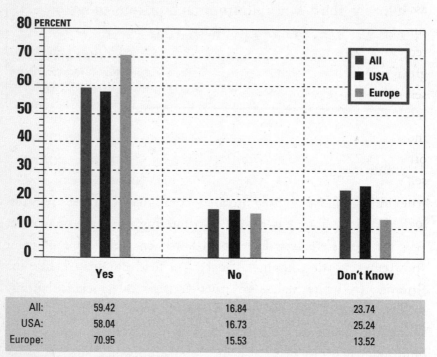

	Yes	No	Don't Know
All:	59.42	16.84	23.74
USA:	58.04	16.73	25.24
Europe:	70.95	15.53	13.52

Internet Demographics (courtesy Georgia Institute of Technology)
The Net does not currently represent a cross-section of the world population, but trends in every category indicate that it is moving in that direction. These figures represent the latest available data available from a series of surveys conducted by Jim Pitkow and Colleen Kehoe at GVU Center, College of Computing, at the Georgia Institute of Technology, Atlanta, GA 30332-0280.

We're often reminded that access to the Net would be superfluous—indeed, some say, meaningless—to a poor family in a Third World country. This is easily true as the world stands today. However, the knowledge and skills of the world's agricultural sciences could be delivered to remote locations via the Net, helping native dwellers to cultivate arid lands, garner better yields from crops and livestock, and learn about medical and social breakthroughs that could better their lives.

Some people are surprised to learn that cellular phones have become widely used in many Third World countries in less time than they've become commonplace in Western countries. This is true despite the fact that these cultures didn't make widespread use of regular landline telephones. The point this example reveals is that assumptions about the irrelevance of technology to emerging cultures may be wrong. Given the opportunity to avail themselves of technological advances, many do so—and those advances sometimes greatly improve their lives. In the case of African villages now being served by cellular telephone service, new technology has enabled remote locations to receive specialized medical, agricultural, and industrial information that they wouldn't have been able to access otherwise. It's also connected them to other communities, giving a sense of a greater "meta-community" within regions. These effects will only be enhanced when Internet service is also available in these locations.

Social Interaction

Once upon a time (at least as recently as a year or two ago), people online generally felt that it was okay to behave in ways they'd never behave in mixed company. This may have reflected the fact that the Net was still primarily a "boys' club," but it was more than that.

There was also a lack of feeling "present" with others (the "presence" we feel in a face-to-face situation). In the absence of facial expressions, vocal cues, and the other conventions that go into the complex process of direct communication, people felt unconstrained.

The combination of these factors in online communication often resulted in the practice known as "flaming"—the exchange of colorful diatribes (mentioned in our earlier discussion of netiquette). Since women and people of color often use language differently than the members of the "Net boys' club," this common practice may have played a role in slowing acceptance of online communication in diverse communities. Certainly, as the Net population has diversified, it's become more and more difficult to base conversation in mutual understanding.

For the most part, the practice of employing aggressive and abusive language has been greatly reduced; flaming is no longer the norm. Those who found it acceptable to attack others in this way in 1992 are now finding themselves reprimanded for flaming, at least in many online communities. Each online service or mailing list or Web community sets and enforces its own standards, however, much the way individuals and institutions do in the physical world. If you don't want to be "bounced" from your favorite chat room, you need to know and abide by the rules there.

Harassment

Another problem scenario—one that exists perhaps only to the extent that it does in society as a whole—is gender-based harassment. In the early days of the Internet, when women made up less than 20 percent of the population online, it was common for a female (using an obviously female name or "handle") to receive unwanted invitations or messages of a sexually explicit nature in chat rooms or via email. These messages, depending on their tone, were comparable to whistles on the street or obscene phone calls.

Many women responded by changing their online identity to a masculine or androgynous name, and usually this solved the problem. Ironically, at the same time, many men found amusement in masquerading as solicitous females, hoaxing males into conversation. Although this practice, along with harassment, undoubtedly continues, it's far less common today than it was just a year or two ago. Most people quickly tire of this kind of playacting and prefer to spend their time cultivating meaningful relationships and obtaining the information they went online to find. In addition, there are many sites and services that cater specifically to women today (see the list at end of the chapter).

Should you find that you're being harassed or abused online (whether you're male or female), you can choose to ignore it—a strategy that often works in the short run. We recommend, however, that you discourage this behavior with a direct request to stop. If the perpetrator doesn't do so, continuing to contact you without your consent, you might try suggestions laid out in the earlier section on spam (for example, filtering unwanted messages and contacting the service provider of the offender). There's no reason to accept behavior that you feel is harassment, regardless of whether the perpetrator intended it to be so.

To avoid both harassment and the *perception* of harassment, take care when approaching someone in an online environment. Make yourself aware of the rules in a given community, and the style that's customary there. If no guideposts are present, exercise caution and refrain from behavior that you wouldn't use if you were face to face.

WEBLINKS TO THIS CHAPTER

computer crime laws by state:

http://eff.org/pub/Social_responsibility/Hacking_cracking_phreaking/
  comp_crime_laws_by_state.list

security issues:

Computer Emergency Response Team: http://www.cert.org/

EFF Hoax Archive: http://www.eff.org/pub/Net_culture/Folklore/Hoaxes/

CIAC Internet Hoax Site: http://ciac.llnl.gov/ciac/CIACHoaxes.html

Platform for Internet Content Selection (PICS): http://www.w3.org/pub/
  www/PICS/

Junk Email Removal Site: http://kenjen.com/nospam/

Get That Spammer!: http://kryten.eng.monash.edu.au/gspam.html

InterNIC WHOIS: http://rs.internic.net/cgi-bin/whois:

National Fraud Information Center: http://www.fraud.org/

For USPS chain-letter information: http://www.usps.gov/websites/
  depart/inspect/chainlet.htm

Computer Security Institute: http://www.gocsi.com/

women's resources online:

http://www.women-online.com/

http://www.women.com/

ethnic resources online:

http://www.netnoir.com/

http://www.blackindex.com/

http://www.latela.com//Welcome.html

http://www.latinoweb.com

http://www.igc.apc.org/acon/

http://www.msw.org/newsletter/index.html

http://microstore.ucs.sfu.ca/StaffPages/MikeStanger/ChineseResources.html

WEBLINKS TO THIS CHAPTER

(cont.)

gay issues online:

http://www.planetout.com/

disability issues online:

http://bucky.aa.uic.edu/#george

SIX | BEYOND THE
FRONTIER

Before the age of electronic communication and digital media, distance and logistics played an imposing, dampening role in the collection and distribution of information. The channels of mass communication were centralized in the hands of publishers and broadcasters. With the advent of the Net, the power of the individual has been greatly increased, forcing society to reevaluate its views on the conflicts between the liberty of individuals and the needs of society. The individual today is empowered not only to share knowledge and creativity in wondrous new ways, but also to infringe the rights of others more freely; misinformation, slander, and invasion of privacy are easier than ever before.

Just a few years ago, the Internet meant nothing to the millions of people who now depend on it for communication, education, and commerce. It doesn't take a crystal ball, then, to see that the Net will be entrenched in our lives tenfold in a decade or two. Because the Internet is a facility built by a human cooperative—a facility that continues to be expanded and remodeled each day—each one of us plays a vital role in its development.

Governments around the world, struggling to deal with this new "place" and its many effects, are scrambling to regulate the Internet. Yet some of those governments (and some of the crucial officials in *all* of those governments) aren't aware of many of the serious issues surrounding the new media—the issues addressed in this book. When they do become aware of them, their first reaction tends to be restriction. This is understandable (with human nature leading us to fear that which we don't understand, we build governments that clamp down on issues that appear to endanger citizens), but it won't work in the new information age.

We're used to having the government act on our behalf, so it seems natural that some governmental body would want to step up and attempt to create the kind of order we've come to expect in our lives. Yet as we've seen, the Internet isn't something that can be physically controlled by government entities as we now know them. Therefore, we must orient ourselves to a new way of thinking about personal and organizational responsibility and appropriate and inappropriate behaviors (and the consequences therefrom).

Within the worldwide community on the Net, subcommunities will develop over time (indeed, have begun to develop already), each with its own particular standards as to what's acceptable, what constitutes a legal transaction, how fraud should be defined, and so on. These standards (or laws, if you prefer) will have a greater moral authority than those that are imposed upon us by a govern-ment—especially for those of us accustomed to a less democratic environment—because they'll be derived from the communities themselves. At the same time, we'll need to have treaties or agreements between governing agencies of the physical world that will enable extradition, so that if an online crime is committed against you in one locality, you'll be able to seek justice from a culprit who lives in another.

This is a critical time for anyone concerned about the utility and regulation of these global networks; we must learn all we can so that we can become involved in their development. The laws and social conventions that are being developed even now for cyberspace will fundamentally affect the lives of generations to come. The issues of cyberspace—an individual's right to speak, the protection of intellectual property, the roles of law enforcement and government, the thorny dilemma of who will have jurisdiction—will be increasingly significant for businesses, individuals, educational institutions, and governments.

Each of us who uses the Net in these formative days is building the foundation of something we can't quite envision; we're not really sure what it can or should become. Why not a place for our highest ideals? As builders, we can choose to create either an environment that supports free expression and association or a place that discourages those values. We should call upon the lessons of history to create a cyber space that extends our physical and intellectual capabilities in new ways while reining in our weaknesses. Since the choice is ours, why not create communities online where compassion and cooperation are basic tenets?

Of *course* it's important for cyberspace to be safe, but at what cost? We can choose to encourage personal responsibility and strong community standards, or we can abdicate our authority, delegating the policing of behavior to governments and supranational organizations. We need to strike a balance between the liberty of individuals and the needs of society, just as we do on the streets of our cities. And the way we can best do that is by learning, using the new media, and making our views on key issues known to everyone from our ISP system administrator to our elected representatives.

As knowledgeable, responsible netizens, we should advocate sensible legislation (or restraint of legislation, where appropriate) that's based on an understanding of the nature and limits of the technologies, as well as of human nature. Since we already have a great many laws on the books, let's use them. Most of those laws apply to cyberspace; a whole new set of laws just for the Internet is neither necessary nor desirable.

Even with a good framework of laws and codes of conduct, we need an effective way to deal with those who violate them. It follows, then, that we would want workable agreements between physical governments so that criminal activity can be investigated and prosecuted, without sacrificing our privacy (or other) rights.

At EFF, we're working to see this happen in a number of ways, with the development of EFF organizations in many countries, each focused on the goals of educating and advocating for protection of rights and responsible behavior online. In addition, we're continuing to pursue programs that foster these objectives, such as the Blue-Ribbon Campaign and TRUSTe.[1] Furthermore, we're working in concert with all interested industry groups and organizations (such as those listed in the Appendix of this book) to maximize our beneficial impact.

With the Internet now representing the largest repository of information ever assembled, you'll understand that we couldn't fit all that you need or want to know in a single book. It's our hope that these pages, along with our Web site (*http://www.eff.org/blueribbon.html*), will serve as a resource and guide to other sources of information on the specific issues of concern to you. And we invite you to become a member of EFF and join us in making history that we can all be proud of.

NOTE

1. The first Blue-Ribbon Campaign, in 1996, was an inaugural program to foster widespread awareness and encourage community action regarding free speech on the Net. Initiated in response to efforts by the U.S. Congress to regulate Internet content, the Campaign promoted a graphic image of a blue ribbon, which would appear on the Web page of any individual or organization that wished to show support for the protection of free speech. The graphic was also a hyperlink to a section of the EFF Web site where users could find the latest information on the issue.

Subsequently, similar campaigns have been launched advocating unrestricted use of cryptography and universal access to Web content.

For more information on TRUSTe (formerly known as eTrust), see the Appendix.

Appendix

"[The Electronic Frontier Foundation] is the undisputed king of electronic civil-liberties groups. It's a veritable powerhouse of news, information, and activism.... EFF doesn't stop at advocacy and news. It boasts an astounding mega-archive.... You can spend hours poking around and come out well-informed on many cyber-liberties issues.... With its high public visibility, authoritative voice, and unbelievably large information warehouse, EFF has perhaps the best issues-oriented site on the Web."

CHRIS TENNEY, *ZDNET/YAHOO!*

This Appendix is intended to give readers an introduction to various organizations formed in the past few years to serve the various needs of communities that intersect and interact online. Each group has a distinctly different mission and approach, although individual goals may be the same in some cases.

We turn first to our own organization.

The Electronic Frontier Foundation (EFF)

To help clarify our role in cyberspace and the public-policy arena, we offer here a partial list of our goals and a roster of some of the concrete ways in which we work toward those goals.

EFF's Goals

- Maintaining our efforts to inform and organize concerned citizens, and to foster directed action on crucial issues such as anticryptographic public-policy mistakes, unconstitutional legislation, ill-considered attempts to greatly expand law enforcement's and intelligence agencies' surveillance capabilities and authority, public access to government information and to communications media, and the unsettled and unsettling intersection of outmoded law and new media.

- Continuing to fight for the privacy of transactional data and to support the use and availability of strong encryption worldwide. Such privacy and security, and the technologies that make them possible, are essential to the continued growth and health of networked communications.

- Encouraging and assisting in the formation of "Electronic Frontiers" civil liberties advocacy groups around the world, and organizing online and offline summits to forge a flexible alliance of grassroots activists acting locally on global issues when necessary, and acting globally on local issues when appropriate.

- Working for the development of legal definitions of the virtual community that are based not on physical location but on the voluntary association of such communities' constituents.

- Establishing a Cyberspace Law Institute to analyze and develop new forms of dispute resolution better adapted to the still-developing jurisdictions of cyberspace.

- Analyzing potential threats and contributions to the Net worldwide and building the information base necessary to produce an annual "State of the Net" report that will study the Internet as an evolving system (using an ecology and organism model).

- Studying the condition of digital intellectual property rights and convening various interested parties to examine how value is currently being, and could be, exchanged online (including, perhaps, a test-bed of digital cash and transaction schemes, with a particular focus on privacy and security issues).

EFF, in conjunction with many other organizations, has formed and participates in a number of coalitions and summits to bring together thinkers from the nonprofit/NGO (Non-Governmental Organization) world, communications and computing industry leaders, government policymakers (when appropriate), and grassroots advocates in a nonpartisan setting to discuss communications policy goals and strategies and to form balanced solutions to problems. Such efforts to date have included the Communications Policy Forum, the Digital Privacy and Security Working Group, and the Intellectual Property Working Group (EFF-organized), as well as the Interactive Working Group and the Stop S.314 Coalition (with EFF as an active participant).

What EFF Does in Support of These Goals

- Works to convince Congress that measures supporting broader public access to information should be enacted into law. EFF supports an Electronic Freedom of Information Act and other legislation to make government information more accessible to citizens.

• Supports both legal and technical means to enhance privacy in communications, advocates measures that ensure the public's right to use the most effective encryption technologies available, and testifies before Congress and conducts online campaigns in support of these issues.

• Works to make sure that common-carriage principles are upheld in the information age. These principles require that network providers carry all speech, regardless of its content. EFF supports a new common-carriage system in which system operators are shielded from liability for the actions of users, but without the regulatory burden presently associated with common carriage.

• Supports an open platform model of the global information infrastructure, providing nondiscriminatory access based on open, private-sector standards and free from burdensome regulation.

• Works to craft policies that enable public and private information providers to distribute and sell their information products over the Internet; encourages the government to provide support for schools, universities, and research labs that buy Internet services on the open market; and works on policies that encourage the government to stimulate the development of experimental, precompetitive network technologies and to fund the development of applications that are helpful to "low-end" users, who are traditionally underserved by advanced digital media.

- Publishes an electronic newsletter, *EFFector Online,* to inform our members and other interested parties (including members of the press, several senators, numerous CEOs of high-technology enterprises, and key staffers in other organizations) about events and issues in online civil liberties and network-based social change.

- Maintains several communications forums on the Internet. We have our own Internet node, which houses our FTP, gopher, and WWW information servers, as well as our own Internet and Usenet conferences, including *comp.eff.org.talk.* We also maintain active conferences on the Whole Earth 'Lectronic Link (WELL), CompuServe (CIS), GEnie, Women's Wire, and elsewhere.

- Answers hundreds of daily Internet-related and civil liberties questions from the community via telephone, postal mail, and email, whether technical ("How do I connect to the Internet?") or legal ("Does my boss have the right to read my email?"). We've built up a strong reputation in the online community as an excellent source of information about life in cyberspace and as the home of the largest archive of online civil liberties information in the world.

Center for Democracy and Technology (CDT)

CDT is a nonprofit public-interest organization. The mission of CDT is to develop public-policy solutions that advance constitutional civil liberties and democratic values in the new computer and communications media. CDT pursues its mission through policy research, public education, and coalition building, marshaling legal, technical, and public-policy expertise on behalf of civil liberties goals. These include maximizing free speech and the free flow of information online, giving citizens more control over personal information, protecting privacy online, and guaranteeing public access to electronic government information.

Info: *info@cdt.org*
General: *ask@cdt.org*
FTP: *ftp.cdt.org, /pub/cdt/*
WWW: *http://www.cdt.org/*
Phone: (202) 637-9800
Fax: (202) 637-0968
Snail: 1001 G Street Northwest, Suite 700E,
    Washington D.C. 20001

Computer Professionals for Social Responsibility (CPSR)

CPSR is a national-membership organization based in Palo Alto, California. CPSR conducts many activities to protect privacy and civil liberties. Membership is open to the public, and support is welcome. CPSR maintains twenty-four local chapters in the United States and has several international affiliates. CPSR hosts several mailing lists, including *cpsr-cpu* (CPSR's "CPU" newsletter for information-technology workers), *cpsr-announce* (CPSR's general news and announcements list, gated to Usenet newsgroup *comp.org.cpsr.announce), bawit-announce* (Bay Area Women and Information Technology working-group announcements), and *cyber-rights* (Cyber-Rights Campaign). CPSR sponsors an annual conference, maintains a large Internet archive site of information, and sponsors working groups on civil liberties and other issues.

Offices:

National headquarters: cpsr@csli.stanford.edu

Washington, D.C., chapter: Larry Hunter—
hunter@nlm.nih.gov

New York chapter: David Friedlander—
friedd@pipeline.com

Berkeley, CA, chapter: Karen Coyle—
cpsr-berkeley@cpsr.org

Palo Alto, CA, chapter: Andre Bacard—
abacard@well.sf.ca.us

Portland, OR, chapter: Erik Nilsson—
erikn@goldfish.mitron.tek.com

Los Angeles chapter: Rodney J. Hoffman—
rodney@oxy.edu

Mailing lists:

listserv@cpsr.org—message body, "subscribe listname [see
above] firstname lastname"

FTP sites:

ftp.cpsr.org, /cpsr
jasper.ora.com, /pub/andyo/cyber-rights/CYBER-RIGHTS/
ftp.iol.ie, /users/rkmoore
WWW: http://www.cpsr.org/home

WWW sites (Cyber-Rights Campaign):

http://www.hotwired.com/special/indecent
http://www.cs.virginia.edu/~hwh6k/public/cyber-rights.html
ftp://ftp.iol.ie/users/rkmoore

UseNet:

comp.org.cpsr.talk, comp.org.cpsr.announce

Electoral issues:
 Eva Waskell, (703) 435-1283 evenings

Snail/phone/fax:
 CPSR *national office, P.O. Box 717, Palo Alto, CA 94302,*
 (650) 322-3778, fax (650) 322-3798

Electronic Privacy Information Center (EPIC)

The Electronic Privacy Information Center is a public-interest research
center in Washington, D.C. It was established in 1994 to focus public
attention on emerging privacy issues relating to the National
Information Infrastructure—issues such as the Clipper Chip, the digital
telephony proposal, medical record privacy, and the sale of consumer
data. EPIC is sponsored by the Fund for Constitutional Government and
Computer Professionals for Social Responsibility. EPIC publishes the
EPIC Alert and *EPIC Reports,* pursues Freedom of Information Act litigation, and conducts policy research on emerging privacy issues. EPIC also
works closely with Privacy International, a human rights group, on
domestic and international privacy issues.

General:
 info@epic.org

FTP sites:
 ftp.cpsr.org, /cpsr/privacy/epic/
 ftp.cpsr.org, /cpsr/alert/

WWW sites:
 http://www.digicash.com
 http://cpsr.org/dox/privacy.html
 http://cpsr.org/cpsr/privacy/epic/
 http://cpsr.org/cpsr/alert/

Snail/phone/fax:
>666 Pennsylvania Avenue Southeast, Suite 301,
>Washington, D.C. 20003, (202) 544-9240,
>fax (202)547-5482

Voters Telecommunications Watch (VTW)

Voters Telecommunications Watch is a volunteer organization dedicated to monitoring federal legislation that affects telecommunications and civil liberties. Based in New York, VTW has volunteers throughout the United States. VTW keeps scorecards on legislators' positions on legislation that affects telecommunications and civil liberties. The group hosts two mailing lists: *vtw-announce* and *vtw-list*.

>General: *vtw@vtw.org*
>Administration: *shabbir@panix.com*
>Press contact: *stc@vtw.org*
>Mailing lists: *listproc@vtw.org*—message body, "subscribe listname
> [see above] firstname lastname"
>Web: *http://www.vtw.org*
>Phone: (718) 596-2851

In addition to the groups listed above and elsewhere in this book, there are numerous local and regional organizations (including independent EFF chapters) in

Master list of online organizations: *http://eff.org/pub/Groups/*

many localities. There are, in fact, too many to list here. You can find a fairly complete list on the EFF Web site at *http://eff.org/pub/Groups/*.

Whom Do You TRUSTe?

In addition to the personal information you keep on file about you and your family—crucial identifying numbers, for example, and medical and financial data—there's another set of facts about you that you may not even be aware of. Web sites you visit, files you download, and specific information about you and your online habits are recorded regularly—with and without your knowledge. Whether it's through the "cookie" that tells your favorite site what you like to do there (and customizes the page for you), the script that tells a Web server what banner advertisement to target at you, or the forms you willingly fill out online, you're disseminating data about yourself whenever you log on.

These tools may serve to make life online more convenient for you (since they do things like remember your passwords and help you find what you're interested in), but they can also be used by marketers or others (including government sites) to develop a profile about you. Have you ever wondered why you're getting the junk email you get? Chances are pretty good the answer has to do with the buying and selling of information about you.

In an ideal digital world, every time information about us was being recorded, we'd be informed about who was doing it, who would use the information, and how it would be used. And we'd have the opportunity to decline interaction, or even negotiate for it ("I'll give you my email address in exchange for access to your great Web site," or "I'll fill out your form for a discount on your widgets"). Of course, this isn't the case today. One of the best things you can do to help civilize the electronic frontier is to tell the people you interact with online how you feel about your personal information; let them know you're concerned about privacy issues; let them know that if they want to build a relationship with you, they need to demonstrate ethical and responsible online policies.

As for the accumulating, buying, and selling of information about you without your consent, there are certain things you can do to minimize these activities. Be aware of the amount and nature of information you intentionally give to Web site operators in forms, and use an encryption program when sending sensitive personal messages. Beyond that, look for "TRUSTe" symbols on commercial Web sites: they're designed to tell you what type of information about you is being gathered, how it will be used, and with whom it will be shared. These symbols are the brainchild of a group called TRUSTe, a broad-based industry and public-interest project to protect privacy and promote security online.

In July of 1996, a group of online commerce pioneers announced the formation of an online transactional security and privacy project, code-named eTrust (later renamed TRUSTe due to a trademark dispute). The organization's goal is to create market incentives for online businesses to adopt a new best-practices consumer privacy model, backed up by the licensing of service marks and auditing of company policies and practices. TRUSTe aims to both improve Internet businesses' information-gathering (and usage) practices and build public confidence in online commerce.

The TRUSTe program licenses symbols ("trustmarks") representing various types of privacy and security to online merchants through an ongoing program of certification and auditing (similar to those of the Better Business Bureau, the Good Housekeeping Institute, and Underwriters Laboratories). The TRUSTe privacy standards define how personal data is collected and what's done with it. The system enables vendors to leverage consumer trust by quickly communicating to customers what personal information is being collected, and to what end. The security guidelines provide a framework to ensure that data isn't compromised by unauthorized access.

Because TRUSTe was designed to provide online merchants with a

clear set of standards and guidelines for security practices, the ultimate beneficiaries of the trustmark program will be online consumers, who will be better able to make informed choices regarding electronic purchasing, Web site browsing, online registration,
and other types of online transactions. "TRUSTe does not make a
judgment about the need or desire to collect information," says
EFF executive director Lori Fena. "Rather, it promotes full disclosure to individuals about how and where that information will be
used."

The key principles for the TRUSTe project include the following:

- *Informed consent is necessary.* Consumers have the right to be
  informed about the privacy and security consequences of an
  online transaction *before* entering into it.

- *There's no privacy without appropriate security.* Privacy and
  security are inexorably linked in an online transaction.
  There's no privacy protection unless there are reliable security measures.

- *Privacy standards vary according to context of use.* No single
  privacy standard is adequate for all situations or all participants.

The TRUSTe project goes beyond simply publishing guidelines of
practices, taking an important first step toward real-world implementation of a visual and quickly comprehensible system, made credible
by a certification process. The TRUSTe visual symbols provide an
instant and reliable guidepost for the fast-paced world of the
Internet.

Ideally, TRUSTe will help cut through a lot of the technical double-
speak that puts consumers off from trusting transactions over the
public networks. With enhanced consumer confidence, the stage will

then be set for the kind of growth the Net is capable of bringing to the businesses represented there.

To participate in the TRUSTe effort, or for more information on the project, please inquire at *truste@truste.org.* Documents regarding the TRUSTe system and the principles underlying it are available at *http://www.TRUSTe.org.*

Contributors

The knowledge, experiences, and opinion in *Protecting Yourself Online* is collected from diverse sources, and distilled to bring the reader practical, usable information about online communication. We want to thank the individuals and organizations that shared their expertise, including:

John Perry Barlow, EFF co-founder, lyricist, rancher
Jordan Breslow, attorney
Esther Dyson, EFF chair, business executive
Lori Fena, EFF executive director
Adam Gaffin, author of EFF *Guide to the Internet*
Beth Givens, director, Privacy Rights Clearinghouse
Mike Godwin, EFF counsel
Mitch Kapor, EFF co-founder
Pamela Samuelson, EFF counsel
Shari Steele, EFF counsel
Jim Warren, author, activist, neighbor of this book's author
Thanks for their editorial assistance:
    Julia Gilden
    Renée Lund
    Wendy Goodfriend

Additional Acknowledgments

We also wish to thank the following organizations for their valuable cooperation:

Privacy Rights Clearinghouse
email: pre@privacyrights.org
web: http://www.privacyrights.org

for use of their factsheets on "Privacy in Cyberspace," "Medical Information Privacy," "Employee Monitoring," "Wireless Communications," and their checklist of responsible information-handling practices.

GeorgiaTech Research Corp., Georgia Institute of Technology
http://www.gvu.gatech.edu
for data on Internet usage

Wired Magazine Group, Inc.
for use of the article "The Economy of Ideas," by John Perry
    Barlow, *Wired* 2.03
info@wired.com
http://www.wired.com

MIT Press
Cambridge, MA
for use of the material from *Everybody's Guide to the Internet,*
    (by Adam Gaffin, MIT Press, 1994)

Scientific American
New York, NY
for use of the article, "Civil Liberties in Cyberspace,"
    by Mitch Kapor

Index

ActiveX, 47

Advanced Research Projects Agency (ARPA), 2–3

agent processing, 70

age of Internet users, 159

agriculture, 10

Amateur Action BBS, 23–24

American Civil Liberties Union (ACLU), 69, 70

America Online (AOL), 39, 87, 116, 126

Andreesen, Mark, 6

anonymous remailers, 61–62, 79, 80

Apache, 58

Apple, 57, 115, 135

applets, 47

Apple v. *Franklin*, 89

archive copy, 90–91

Arms Export Control Act, 57–58

ARPANet, 2, 3

art, 8, 60, 87–88, 91

ASCII text, 122

Asia, 49, 99, 107, 108

audience, 119, 120

baby monitors, 72, 74

Baker, Jake, 28, 32*n*.3

banking, 9, 48, 81, 147

Barlow, John Perry, xii, 13, 28, 39, 104, 107

BBS (bulletin-board system), 23–24, 25, 30, 39, 41, 131–34

Behlendorf, Brian, 58

Berman, Jerry, xii

Berne Convention for the Protection of Literary and Artistic Works (1886), 105, 106, 113*n*.4

Berners Lee, Tim, 6

Bernstein, Daniel, 55–59

Bernstein v. *U.S. Department of State*, 54–60

Bill of Rights, 19, 20, 21, 135

Blue-Ribbon Campaign, 172, 173*n*.1

bots, 6
Brandenburg v. *Ohio*, 138–39
browsers, 6
browsing Web sites, 44–46
bulk-class mail, 129
business data, 9–11, 171; safeguarding, 38, 64–71

Canada, 49
cell sites, 72
cellular phones, xvi, 1, 163; digital,
   73, 74; privacy issues, 37, 63,
   71–75, 81
censorship online, and free expression, 19–33
Center for Democracy and
   Technology (CDT), xii, 179–80
chain letters, 151–54
character limitations, 122
chat, 42
children, 7, 26, 79, 116; Internet
   protection, 26, 32*nn*.2, 4, 33*n*.4,
   79; pornography, 23–24, 25, 26,
   27, 30
China, 108
Church of Scientology, 30, 61
Cisler, Steve, 115
civil liberties, 10, 28, 131–41, 176,
   179, 180
clickstream information, 45–46
clickwrap license, 96
Clinton, Bill, 52
Clipper Chip, 54–56
Cohn, Cindy, 59
Cold War, 50, 51
colleges, 3, 10–11
common-carriage principles, 178
Communications Decency Act
   (CDA), 27, 30, 32*n*.4, 33*n*.4

community standards, 23–25, 26,
   30
CompuServe, 4, 39, 87, 116, 126
Computer Emergency Response
   Team, 148
computer monitoring, 66–67
computer networking, history of,
   1–3
Computer Professionals for Social
   Responsibility (CRSP), 180–82
Computers, Freedom, and Privacy
   Conference, xii
Computer Security Institute, 70
conduct, online, 115–67, 172;
   hacking and cracking, 130–46,
   147; information warfare,
   146–47; issues in online equality,
   157–65; netiquette, 117–23;
   scams, 149–57; social interaction, 163–64; spam, 123–28,
   129; spoofing, 128–30; symbology, 122–23; viruses, 147–49,
   154–57
Congress, U.S., 19, 32*n*.4, 33*n*.4,
   37, 57, 69, 96, 100, 173*n*.1,
   177–78
Constitution, U.S., 19, 20, 57, 89,
   132, 134
constitutional issues, 14–15, 16,
   19–33, 53, 54–50, 132–41, 176,
   179
content, 86, 116
cookies, 44–46, 184
Copyright Act, 89, 103
Copyright Office, U.S., 92, 94, 103
copyrights, 27, 87–97, 103,
   104–106, 107, 108, 121, 138,
   139, 140; evolution of copyright
   law, 89–91; fair-use doctrine,

96–97; jurisdictional confusion, 104–106; modification of copyrighted digital media, 91–92; notice, 92–93; protection, 88–97; transferring, 94–95

cordless phones, xvi, 63, 71–74, 81; digital, 73

courts, xii; encryption and, 54–60

cracking, 130–31

credit cards, 54, 76, 78; privacy issues, 26, 27, 37, 38, 72, 135, 138, 143

crediting sources, 121

crime and fraud, xix, 10, 18, 23–25, 27, 37–38, 46, 54, 71–75, 124, 127–29, 150, 171; hacking and cracking, 130–46, 147; scams, 149–57

cultural barriers, 162–63, 164

Cyber-Cash, 60

cyberspace, xix, 1, 5, 9, 13–18, 27, 107, 171; privacy in, 39–40, 76–79

cyber-terrorism, 146–47

Dalzell, Justice, 27

database protection, 102–104

data security, 70, 71

defamation, 27, 28

democracy, 19

Diffie, Whitfield, 50

Digital Equipment Corporation, 143

digital media, xviii, 1, 7, 8, 87

direct marketers, 41, 78

disabled Internet users, 159–61

disk monitoring, 66

domain names, 98–101, 112n.1, 113n.1

driver's licenses, 54

Dyson, Esther, 19, 85, 87

education, 10–11

EFFector Online, 179

Electronic Communications Privacy Act (ECPA), 42–43, 139

Electronic Frontier Foundation (EFF), xi-xiii, xx, xxii, xxiii, 12, 16, 17, 18, 38, 53, 54–60, 70, 110, 132, 172, 175, 176–79; goals, 176–79

Electronic Privacy Information Center (EPIC), 182–83

electronic serial number (ESN), 74

email, xx, xxii, 2, 3, 5, 11, 27, 29, 87, 117, 118, 131; birth of, 2; encryption, 47–50, 61–62, 68–69, 79; junk, 41, 44, 78, 79, 123–28; monitoring, 67–69; netiquette, 117–23; privacy issues, 39–46, 64, 67–69, 75, 76–79, 80, 81; spoofing, 128–30; workplace, 42

encryption, 47–62, 68–69, 71, 77, 79, 83nn.3–5, 128, 129, 145, 176, 178; Clipper Chip, 54–56; courts and, 54–60; history of, 49–56

equality, online, 157–65

Europe, 99, 106, 107, 146, 147

European Particle Physics Laboratory (CERN), 6

export-control laws, 55–60

extortion, 27

extradition issues, 30–31

fair-use doctrine, 96–97

false security, 106–11

fax, 63
fax-bombing, 125
Federal Bureau of Investigation (FBI), xii, 15, 28, 51, 52, 101, 128, 140, 144
Federal Communications Commission, 75
Federal Networking Council (FNC), 99
Fena, Lori, xii, xv
fictitious virus announcements, 154–57
filtering software, 32n.2, 46, 70
finger technology, 41
First Amendment, 19, 21, 22, 24, 27, 30, 55–60, 132, 134, 136, 137
flaming, 11, 117, 118, 164
Fourth Amendment, 134, 139, 140
fraud, 10, 18, 27, 71–75, 124–29, 150; *see also* crime and fraud
freedom of the press, 19–26; consequences of widespread, 22–26
free speech, 14, 19–22, 27–31, 38, 55–60, 132–38, 173n.1; censorship online and, 19–22; online limits, 27–31
FTP sites, 44, 117
future of the Internet, 7–18, 169–73

gender-based harassment, 164–65
gender of Internet users, 158, 159, 161, 164–65
General Atomics, 112n.1
Gibson, William, 13
Gilmore, John, xii, 16, 22, 59, 110
Gingrich, Newt, 161
global community, 50–51, 57, 100, 105–106, 170–71, 178; and free speech, 30–31

Godwin, Mike, 23
Good Times virus, 155–56, 157
Gopher, 5
government, xxii, 3, 9, 11–12, 16, 17, 19, 30–31, 36, 37, 38, 46, 49, 52, 54–60, 170–71, 177–78
guarding frontier outposts, 12–18
Gulf War, 146–47

hacking and cracking, 130–46, 147
harassment, 27, 78, 164–65
hard-drive intrusions, 47
Harlan, John M., 35
headers, 121; checking, 121; stripping, 121
headsets, 65–66
hoaxes, 150–57
Holland, 30–31
Hong Kong, 29
Hormel Foods Corporation, 123, 124
HTML (Hypertext Markup Language), 6
human rights, 8
humor and sarcasm, 120

IBM, 57
identity, 14, 41, 54, 78–79, 88, 171; theft, 38, 83n.2
idle-time monitoring, 67
income, average annual household, 160–63
individual rights, 8–9, 14, 19–33, 171; safeguarding personal data, 35–83
information warfare, 146–47
insurance companies, 63
intellectual property, 7, 27, 60–61, 86, 140, 171, 177; copyrights,

87–97, 103, 104–106, 107, 108;
definition of, 86–87; false security, 106–11; jurisdictional confusion, 104–106; original database protection, 102–104; protection, 60–61, 85–113; trademarks and patents, 87, 97–102,
107, 108, 113n.3
intellectual value, 86
interactivity, xx
International Telecommunication
Union (ITU), 99
International Trademark
Association (INTA), 99
International Traffic in Arms
Regulations (ITAR), 55–59
Internet, xxii, 1, 3; birth and
growth of, xvii, 1–3, 18; free
expression and censorship
online, 19–33; future of, 7–18,
169–73; privacy and anonymity,
33–85; responsible conduct on,
115–67, 172; workings of, 4–6
Internet Architecture Board (IAB),
99
Internet Assigned Numbers
Authority (IANA), 99
Internet International Ad Hoc
Committee (IHAC), 99
Internet service provider (ISP), 29,
31, 39, 116–17, 126–27; privacy
and, 40–47, 76–78
Internet Society (ISOC), 99
InterNIC, 100, 101, 112n.1,
113n.1

Jackson, Steve, xii, 131–33, 139
Japan, 49, 99
Java, 6, 47

Junkbusters, 46
junk mail, 41, 44, 78, 79, 123–28
jurisdictional confusion, 104–106

Kapor, Mitch, xii, 13, 109, 131
Kashpureff, Eugene, 100–101
keystroke monitoring, 66

labeling, 70
legal issues, xxi, 7, 11–12, 13,
14–15, 16, 23, 32n.4, 33n.4,
36–37, 42–43, 62, 170, 172,
176–78; copyrights, 87–97;
encryption, 54–60; free speech
and, 27–31; hacking and cracking, 130–46; intellectual property and, 85–113
legislators, 11–12, 16, 17, 37, 69,
81, 172, 177–78
Lehman, Bruce, 85
licenses, 95–96
line length, 122
listservers, 40–41, 80
logic bombs, 146
Lotus, 135

mail-bombing, 125
market value, 86
Markoff, John, *Cyberpunk*, 143
mass communication, redefining,
20–22
medical privacy, 37, 62–64, 80–81
member directories, 41
Microsoft, 57, 135
micro-transactions, 60
military, 50, 146–47
Miller v. *California*, 24, 25, 37
mistakes, 121–22
Mitnick, Kevin, 26, 141–45

mobile identification number
    (MIN), 74
modem, 3, 4, 23
Mosaic, 6
music, 8, 60, 88, 92

NASA Jet Propulsion Laboratory,
    Pasadena, 143
NASD Regulation, Inc., 150
National Center for Computer
    Crime Data, 148
National Computer Security
    Association, 70
National Science Foundation,
    112n.1
National Security Agency (NSA),
    52, 58
Netcom Internet Services, 143, 145
netiquette, 117–23
network security, 70
newsletters, online, 40
news media, xxi, xxii, xxiii, 7, 12,
    21, 136
Norton UnErase, 68
NSI, 98, 99, 113nn.1, 2
nuclear attack, 32n.1

obscenity, 24–25, 27, 28, 29,
    33n.4, 136, 164
online monitoring, 67
Operation Sun Devil, 15, 16
organizations, 175–83
original database protection,
    102–104

PacBell, 141, 142, 143
packet switching, 2
pagers, 1; privacy, 71–72
Parmenter, Tom, 91

passports, 54
passwords, 37, 48, 55, 71, 77, 78,
    128–29, 130
Patel, Marilyn Hall, 57–59
patents, 87, 101–102, 107, 108,
    113n.3
pen register, 66
personal communication service
    (PCS) devices, 75
personal data, 8–9, 14, 19–33, 171;
    safeguarding, 35–83
phone-flooding, 125
photography, 88, 93
Photoshop, 92
Phrack, 133
pirated domains, 98
plagiarism, 88
police, xii, 26
Popular Mechanics, xvii
pornography, xix, xxi, 18, 22,
    23–25, 26, 27, 30
postal services, 7
Pretty Good Privacy (PGP), 46, 49,
    51, 57, 83n.6
privacy and security issues, xviii,
    xxii, 7, 8–10, 18, 33–85, 171,
    176, 182, 184–87; anonymous
    remailers, 61–62; browsing Web
    sites, 44–46; cellular phones, 37,
    63, 71–75; computer monitor-
    ing, 66–67; cordless phones,
    71–74; encryption, 47–62,
    68–69, 71, 77, 79, 128, 145,
    176, 178; hacking and cracking,
    130–46, 147; hard-drive intru-
    sions, 47; individual rights,
    35–83; intellectual property,
    60–61, 85–113; medical privacy,
    37, 62–64, 80–81; organiza-

tions, 81–82; pager, 71–72; private areas, 42–44; protection tools and strategies, 76–81; public areas, 40–41; semi-private areas, 41–42; telephone, 65–66, 71–75, 81; workplace, 64–71, 81, 171

Privacy Protection Act (1980), 139

private areas, 42–44

Prodigy, 4, 126

proxy server, 46

public areas, 40–41

public domain, 90, 92, 98–101, 121

public key cryptography, 48–49, 50, 83*n*.5

radio scanners, 72–73

rating, 70

remailers, anonymous, 61–62, 79, 80

reposted messages, 120

responsible conduct, *see* conduct, online

Rogers, Alara, 31

ROM, 89

Rome Convention for the Protection of Performers, Producers of Phonograms, and Broadcasting Organizations, 106

Rural Telephone v. *Feist Publications*, 103–104

scams, 149–57

screen monitoring, 66

search-indexing, 70

Secret Service, 15, 18*n*.1, 131–32, 140

security, *see* privacy and security issues

semi-private areas, 41–42

service provider, *see* Internet service provider (ISP)

Shenk, David, *Data Smog*, xvii

Shergold, Craig, 151

Shimomura, Tsutomu, 144, 145

shrinkwrap license, 95, 96

signature, 49, 122

Simple Mail Transfer Protocol (SMTP), 129

Singapore, 29–30, 61

Smart-Cards, 60

social interaction, 163–64

Social Security number, 78

Software Act (1980), 89, 90, 91

spam, 11, 41, 44, 78, 79, 123–28, 129; fighting, 125–28

speed, 4, 5

spelling, 119, 121

spoofing, 128–30

stalking, 78

Statute of Anne, 89

Steele, Shari, 55, 59

Steve Jackson Games, 131–33, 139

stripping headers, 121

subject lines, 119

submarine patents, 102

Sun, 57

symbology, 122–23

sysop, 40, 43, 44, 76, 78, 137, 138

technological progress, xv-xxiii, 15, 162–63, 169–73

telephone, 21, 43, 63, 64; cellular, xvi, 1, 37, 63, 71–75, 81; cordless, xvi, 63, 71–74, 81; headsets, 65–66; privacy issues, 65–66, 71–75, 81; records, 66

television, 22

Telnet, 5
Tenney, Chris, 175
terrorism, cyber-, 146–47
text format, 122
theft, xxi, 37–38, 71, 83*n*.2,
    100–101, 106; *see also* crime and
    fraud; privacy and security issues
Third World, 163
Thomas, Robert and Carleen,
    23–24, 30, 37
Tien, Lee, 59
Time magazine, 20
Toffler, Alvin, *The Third Wave*, 109
trademarks, 87, 97–102
training, 161–63
transfer of copyright, 94–95
TRUSTe, 172, 173*n*.1, 184–87
2600 (magazine), 18*n*.1

U.S. Privacy Protection Study
    Commission (1977), 24, 35
Universal Copyright Convention,
    89
University of Michigan, 28
Usenet groups, 28, 117, 119–22,
    127–28
user directory, 5

video, 23
virtual communities, 23–25
viruses, xxi, 147–49; fictitious virus
    announcements, 154–57
voicemail, 64, 81; monitoring,
    67–69

Voters Telecommunications Watch
    (VTW), 183

WAIS (Wide Area Information
    Search), 5
WarGames (movie), 135
Warren, Jim, 157
watermark, 92
WebFilter, 46
WELL (Whole Earth 'Lectronic
    Link), 88, 144, 145
WIPO Copyright Treaty, 106
WIPO Performances and
    Phonograms Treaty, 106
wireless communications, privacy
    of, 37, 63, 71–75, 81
work for hire, 95
workplace, transfer of copyright at,
    94–95
workplace privacy, 64–71, 81, 171;
    protection, 69–71
World Intellectual Property
    Organization (WIPO), 99, 106,
    113*n*.4
World Wide Web, xx, xxii, 6, 30,
    39, 47, 67, 77, 79, 93, 98, 117,
    119, 184; browsing Web sites,
    44–46
writing, 88, 93, 94

YOYOW (You Own Your Own
    Words), 88

Zimmerman, Phil, 51, 52

About the Author

Robert Gelman is a writer, editor, musician, interactive media developer, and event producer, with his roots in the performing arts. His company, BG and Associates, provides audio and other content for companies such as Mindscape Entertainment, Disney, and America Online.

He serves as a contributing editor to *InterActivity Magazine* and is a regular contributor to newspapers and journals on subjects of interest to interactive media developers.

He was co-founder and producer of the seminal CyberArts International conferences and festivals, producer of the Digital Be-In, and dozens of other live high-technology events. He also serves as a consultant to other event producers. He is a judge for the Global Information Infrastructure Awards and is a fellow of the Seybold Institute.

For those interested in a digest of views from many corners about cyber-rights and responsibilities, he offers a free email-delivered newsletter, which can be subscribed-to by sending him an email request at: *cyberguy@bgamedia.com*.